T0053849

a SAVOR THE SOUTH *cookbook*

Sweet Potatoes

a SAVOR THE SOUTH *cookbook*

Sweet
Potatoes

APRIL McGREGER

The University of North Carolina Press CHAPEL HILL

© 2014 April McGreger
All rights reserved.
Designed by Kimberly Bryant and set in Miller and
Calluna Sans types by Rebecca Evans.

The paper in this book meets the guidelines for permanence and durability of
the Committee on Production Guidelines for Book Longevity of the Council on
Library Resources.

Cover illustration courtesy of John Gollop/Getty Images.

Library of Congress Cataloging-in-Publication Data
McGreger, April.
Sweet potatoes / April McGreger.
pages cm. — (Savor the South cookbooks)
Includes bibliographical references and index.
ISBN 978-1-4696-1766-4 (cloth : alk. paper)
ISBN 978-1-4696-7749-1 (pbk. : alk. paper)
ISBN 978-1-4696-1767-1 (ebook)
1. Cooking (Sweet potatoes)
2. Cooking, American—Southern style. I. Title.
TX803.S94M39 2014   641.6′522—dc23   2014009212

The Sweet Potato Grits recipe in this book is reprinted with permission from
Virginia Willis, *Basic to Brilliant, Y'all: 150 Refined Southern Recipes and Ways
to Dress Them Up for Company* (Berkeley: Ten Speed Press, 2011), © 2011; for
more information, visit www.virginiawillis.com.

To my father, Earl McGreger,

nurturer of field, family, and community

Contents

Mains, Soups, Stews, and In-Betweens 71
A WORLD OF FLAVOR

Desserts **101**

A LITTLE SOMETHING SWEET

a SAVOR THE SOUTH *cookbook*

Sweet Potatoes

Introduction

Sweet potatoes are as rampant as the kudzu vine all over the South.
— Betty Fussell, *I Hear America Cooking*

ertain foods are of such significance to my identity that
I am bound and determined to pass on a love for them
to my son. He will love field peas; he will love cornbread; he will love okra and chicken and dumplings
and boiled peanuts; and he will love sweet potatoes.
These foods are not just important to me; they *are* me. In serving my son these foods, I am passing on a love for them that is
greater than a love of the way they taste. In the wise words of
New Orleans's passionate cooking teacher and culinary historian
Poppy Tooker, we have to "eat it to save it." We are not only saving
such foods but also passing on our cultural identity to the next
generation in the process. And is there any food more central to
our southern identity than sweet potatoes?

The sweet potato was of such importance in the pastoral Piney
Woods of Mississippi in 1840 that a traveler noted that it was the
only crop cultivated in this region of poor white cattle and hog
grazers. It was so versatile and dependable that it was the only
crop needed. It was reported that the traveler "ate sweet potatoes
with wild turkeys and various other meats, had a potato pie for
dessert and roasted potatoes offered to him as a side dish, drank
sweet potato coffee and sweet potato home brew, had his horse
fed on sweet potatoes and sweet potato vines, and when he retired he slept on a mattress stuffed with sweet potato vines and
dreamed he was a sweet potato someone was digging up."

A life so dependent on one crop may be difficult to fathom, but
not much has changed in my hometown of Vardaman, Mississippi, in the nearly 175 years since that time. It is a place where the
sweet potato is not just a southern food but the center of a whole
network of ties to community, economics, and identity. The annual Sweet Potato Festival, held on the first Saturday in Novem-

ber, culminates a weeklong celebration of the annual harvest with sweet potato–cooking contests, tasting booths offering everything from sweet potato sausage balls to sweet potato bonbons, and, in true southern fashion, a Sweet Potato Queen.

As the daughter and sister of sweet potato farmers in the self-proclaimed Sweet Potato Capital of the United States, I consider sweet potatoes a mainstay of my family dinner table. In addition to sustenance, they have provided their share of life lessons. By the time I was a teenager, I had worked at pulling slips, the shoots that densely bedded "seed" sweet potatoes send up, and had spent a couple of summers riding the "setter" that plants those sweet potato slips in expansive fields. I learned firsthand how eyes and ears and noses fill with dust from the warm, just-plowed earth and how the modern farmer's schedule is set by nature and financial demands, often at odds with each other. By then I knew, too, of the sweet potato's versatility in the kitchen and that, after a few early failures in pursuit of the "Little Miss Sweet Potato Queen" title , I was more apt to win my sweet potato accolades there than on the pageant stage.

It is a southern tradition to have a story for everything, and the sweet potato delivers a fascinating one. All southerners—rich or poor, black or white—owe no less than their lives to it. During and after the Civil War, sweet potatoes are said to have saved both rich and poor from starvation. Without a doubt, they also provided long-term nutrition to the region's poorest residents, both black and white.

In the story of the sweet potato, we find the themes of loss and redemption that run through much of southern culture. Once such a prominent food in the southern diet, the sweet potato is now eaten by many only on Thanksgiving in the form of sweet potato casserole or sweet potato pie. There was a time in recent history that it would have been embarrassing to admit to enjoying sweet potatoes (and many other lowly foodstuffs such as ramps, grits, collard greens, and chitlins) in educated and middle-class circles. Luckily, times are changing. There is an increasing awareness and valuing of traditional, local foods and a rejection of homogeneity and globalization. A rising tradition of southern chefs starting with the late Edna Lewis and Bill Neal celebrates these seemingly pedestrian southern foods. Food writer John T. Edge sees these themes as part of a larger consciousness of the value of community, which results in "knitting back together the tethers of community by way of food."

George Washington Carver said that sweet potatoes were one of "the greatest gifts God has ever given us" and claimed they had the potential to replenish soils ravaged by King Cotton. Might it finally be time to take heed of this wisdom?

Early History of the Sweet Potato: Origins and Discovery

The sweet potato was grown in the southeastern United States long before the first Europeans arrived. De Soto found sweet potatoes being cultivated by Native Americans in Louisiana and as far north as Georgia in 1540. By 1648, the Virginia colonists were growing them. The Native American provenance of sweet potatoes is reflected in an early recipe resembling sweet potato spoonbread that appears in *The Carolina Housewife* under its Indian name, Espetanga Corn Bread.

Archaeological evidence suggests that the sweet potato was domesticated in the Americas at least as far back as 2000 B.C. and possibly as early as 8000 B.C. The latter possibility would make sweet potatoes the earliest major crop planted anywhere in the world. The first known European discovery of sweet potatoes was when Columbus found them growing in Haiti in 1492 and transported them back to Spain, thus making them one of the earliest New World foods adopted in Europe. They were called by their Arawak name *batata*, or in Spanish, *patata*, and eventually, in English, "potato."

Before we can further explore the sweet potato's history, we must first attempt to define what a sweet potato is and clarify what it is not.

The Sweet Potato Incognito

The history of the sweet potato is as tangled as a mass of its twining, trailing vines in late summer. Despite all of the confusion, the sweet potato (*Ipomoea batatas*) is related to neither the russet potato (*Solanum tuberosa*) nor the true African yam (*Dioscorea*). The sweet potato is a member of the morning glory family, and if you have ever laid eyes on the plant, you have seen the similarities. The only food plant in this family, it is actually a swollen storage root and a storehouse of nutrients. The ordinary russet potato, however, is technically not a root but a subterranean tuber, but it is also of New World origin. The true African yam is a large, hairy tuber of tropical origins related to neither the russet potato nor the sweet potato, and it has only recently been imported to the United States and sold in African specialty markets.

The centuries of gastronomic and botanical confusion between the yam and the sweet potato began with the slave trade. Ships transporting enslaved Africans to America were provisioned with true yams. In America, there were no yams, so they were replaced with sweet potatoes, a New World crop common in "Indian gardens." Slaves even took to calling them by the West African word *nyami*, which was Anglicized to "yam."

The confusion was further compounded in the 1930s when the USDA allowed Louisiana to brand the moist, bright orange Puerto Rican variety of sweet potato as a yam, however incorrect that designation may be. By capitalizing on its traditional name, Louisiana hoped to distinguish its sweet potato from the then prevalent paler, drier varieties grown in Virginia, Maryland, and New Jersey. Fast-forward to today when those varieties are grown nationwide, and there is anarchy in the produce department.

The linguistic imbroglio involving the sweet potato and the russet potato occurred when the Spanish encountered *Solanum tuberosa* in South America in 1529, nearly forty years after discovering the sweet potato. They called russet potatoes *batatas* as well because they reminded them of sweet potatoes, which they had already come to love.

If I have learned one thing as I have researched the history of the sweet potato, it is how often the authors themselves have been befuddled. *The Oxford English Dictionary* states that in his 1597 book, *Herball*, John Gerard called white potatoes "Virginia Potatoes" and later "Bastard Potatoes." In *Food*, Waverly Root asserts that Gerard must have been speaking of sweet potatoes for russet potatoes did not exist in Virginia, or anywhere in North America, at this time.

Flip through any historical southern cookbook like *The Carolina Housewife* or *The Virginia House-wife*, and I challenge you to determine which "potato" the author is referencing. You will find recipes for "white potatoes" that call for them to be baked in a sweet pudding seasoned with cinnamon.

In *The Encyclopedia of American Food and Drink*, John F. Mariani tells us that the term "sweet potato" was not used at all in America until the 1740s. It was needed to distinguish sweet potatoes from common white potatoes, which were making increasing claims upon the word "potato" after being introduced by Irish immigrants in Boston around 1719. It is known that *Solanum tuberosum* did not become widely accepted until it received Thomas Jefferson's seal of approval in 1802, when he served "potatoes in the French manner," that is, French fries, to White House guests.

In the South in 1930, the sweet potato had yet to relinquish its title to *Solanum tuberosum*, according to Blanch S. Rhett in *Two Hundred Years of Charleston Cooking*. "If you ask for potatoes in the South you get sweet potatoes. When you want the white tuber of the North you must ask for Irish potatoes," she wrote. In my own experience, older generations of southerners to this day refer to white potatoes as Irish potatoes, or in the local dialect, "Arsh taters." And the word "potatoes," or "taters," is used to refer to either white potatoes or sweet potatoes.

Confusion extends to popular culture as well. In his 1949 hit, Little Jimmy Dickens laments the common predicament of his generation, who as whining, hungry children were told to "take an old cold tater and wait." Dickens is a native of the Appalachian Mountains, the one southern region where *Solarum tuberosa* is of greater significance historically than the sweet potato due to its cooler climate. However, he did not pen the song. The song was written by E. M. Bartlett, who was born in Missouri in 1885 and raised in Arkansas at a time when sweet potatoes would have been much more common both in fields and on tables. Perhaps even more telling, though, is the fact that the song was never meant to be a country song but was written for the comedic jazz quartets of the 1920s. These earliest jazz recordings tended to portray black musicians in a less-than-flattering light. To understand African American history is to understand that the "tater" here surely must have been a sweet potato.

From Slave Quarters to the Big-House Table: Sweet Potatoes in History

In *Seaboard Slave States*, Frederick Law Olmsted suggests that slaves ate a more balanced, healthier diet than most whites, including planters. Despite their meager rations, there is shockingly little evidence of nutritional diseases among slaves. This is likely due to the consumption of the sweet potatoes and greens that slaves grew themselves. Sweet potatoes were preserved through the winter by mounding them in hills and covering them with straw and soil to protect them from frost. The potatoes became sweet and tasty in these curing mounds or "tater hills." Slaves' self-provisioning was often encouraged by their masters not only because it was cost-effective but also because it was discovered that "Negroes fed on three-quarters of a pound of bread and bacon are more prone to disease than if with less meat but with vegetables."

Sweet potatoes took longer to mature, so they were less important to the pioneer than faster-growing crops. However, they were of primary importance to the settled farmer. After sweet potatoes were planted in late spring, hungry children were scratching them out of the ground and eating them raw by midsummer. The sweet potatoes continued to grow and multiply all summer until the main harvest just before frost. Sweet potatoes produced a good yield even in poor, sandy soils, making them a boon for the poorest farmers. In addition, sweet potatoes provided food for livestock, who were fattened before the slaughter with the produce gathered by gleaning the fields after harvest.

By the mid-nineteenth century, southern planters no longer considered sweet potatoes the food of slaves. *The Carolina Housewife*, *The Virginia House-wife*, and *The Kentucky Housewife* all include numerous recipes featuring sweet potatoes. On a tobacco plantation in Petersburg, Virginia, in the mid-nineteenth century, Frederick Law Olmsted reported, "There was . . . but one vegetable served—sweet potato, roasted in ashes, and this, I thought was the best sweet potato, also, I had ever eaten." This food was no doubt placed on the big-house table by the hands of African slaves.

On the eve of the Civil War, the diet of black and white southerners had become homogeneous. Sweet potatoes were listed as one of the most requested foods by both black and poor white southern troops. The sweet potato was invaluable to every class of southerner during wartime. Its underground habit made it less susceptible to deliberate destruction than other crops such as corn or field peas, and it was often the last defense against starvation. It has been said that southerners brought starvation on themselves when they abandoned growing corn and sweet potatoes for a cotton monoculture. This greatly increased southerners' dependence on imported food. When the Civil War began, many agricultural leaders in the South asked farmers to show their support for the Confederacy by replacing cotton with edible crops. Arkansas and Georgia went so far as to pass laws aimed at diversifying agriculture and restricting the cultivation of King Cotton, but by and large these efforts failed. Confederate soldiers were said to have gone days at a time without food, and as a result, they became excellent foragers and scavengers, often feasting on farmers' sweet potato lots that they discovered. They were particularly crazy for anything green, and sweet potato greens were highly prized.

Fifty years later, the pre-industrial South was thick with the aroma of sweet potatoes cooking in woodstoves. Fieldworkers, children, and hunters carried sweet potatoes in their pockets or aprons for a midday meal.

Sweet Potatoes Inspire Great Works

The sweet potato has remained emblematic of African American foodways in the centuries since slavery, and it has served as inspiration for black artists. Novelist Richard Wright claims the first sentence he ever penned while writing his famed autobiography was "The soft melting hunk of butter trickled in gold down the stringy grooves of the split yam."

The sweet potato became a symbol of the freedom obtained through embracing one's cultural identity in Ralph Ellison's *Invisible Man*. The protagonist is overcome with homesickness and memories of shame after an encounter with an old black man selling roasted sweet potatoes out of a cart on the cold streets of Harlem in the 1940s. He remembers, "At home we'd bake them in the hot coals of the fireplace, had carried them cold to school for lunch, munched them secretly, squeezing the sweet pulp from the soft peel as we hid from the teacher behind the largest book, the World's Geography."

As he eats his sweet potato with relish and then goes back for seconds and thirds, he reaffirms his identity, his blackness, and his southern roots by embracing his love for the sweet potato. He declares, "I yam what I am!"

Beyond their common association with soul food, sweet potatoes were actually referenced in its conception. Amiri Baraka, formerly LeRoi Jones, is considered by many to have first used the term "soul food" in *Home: Social Essays* in 1966. In an essay on soul food published as a rebuttal to critics claiming that African Americans had no language or characteristic cuisine, Baraka wrote, "No characteristic food? Oh, man, come on. . . . Sweet potato pies, a good friend of mine asked me recently, 'Do they taste anything like pumpkin?' Negative. They taste more like memory."

Losing Our Roots

In spite of its history and the nostalgia it inspires, the sweet potato has slowly lost its prominent position in the diet of southerners. The per capita consumption of sweet potatoes in the United

States was thirty-one pounds in 1920; by 2000 it had dipped below four pounds. Worldwide statistics show that as a population becomes less impoverished and stops growing its own food, the consumption of sweet potatoes decreases.

There are many explanations for this trend. Modern diets offer more variety and competition, and certainly class plays a role in determining what people eat—and do not eat. Class preferences probably explain why the sweet potato dishes that remain popular are the overly rich ones. My grandfather eventually refused to eat simply baked sweet potatoes, but he relished pies and marshmallow-topped casseroles. After years of eating several baked or raw sweet potatoes a day on a Mississippi family farm, he had had his fill.

This only tells part of the story, however. Today, most of the sweet potatoes grown and consumed in North America are still cultivated in the Southeast, especially in North Carolina, Mississippi, and Louisiana. The sweet potato patch has given way to large sweet potato fields, and the potato hill has been replaced with modern sweet potato storage houses. The decline in sweet potato consumption corresponds with the rise of industrialized agriculture and mechanization, for which the sweet potato is poorly suited. Whereas the russet potato is machine planted and dug, the sweet potato is easily bruised and cannot withstand the rough handling of machine digging and sorting. Thus, the sweet potato industry relies heavily on labor. In the rural areas where sweet potatoes are grown, this seasonal labor can be difficult to find. As a result, skilled migrant labor is essential to the industry. The process of contracting with the U.S. government for migrant labor is difficult and cumbersome and is currently under threat of stricter immigration laws.

The sweet potato is what you eat when you grow your own food. But in the market, the substantial labor involved translates into the higher cost of sweet potatoes. Even more important, the higher cost of production means that there is less desire to turn the sweet potato into a processed or value-added food. In Asia, sweet potatoes are processed into flour and starch and made into noodles of exceptional quality. Japan turns sweet potatoes into the prized liquor known as Shochu. George Washington Carver developed 107 different sweet potato products, yet nearly 100 years later, virtually none of these products have made it out of Carver's lab.

Superfood of the Future

In recent years, the per capita consumption of sweet potatoes has bounced back, up from 3.8 pounds in 2000 to 5.3 pounds in 2011. The reason for the rise in popularity has been the increasing recognition of the sweet potato's health benefits, including its being named the most nutritious vegetable in an extensive study by the Center for Science in the Public Interest in 1992.

The sweet potato is a source of complex carbohydrates, high fiber, vitamins C and B6, calcium, protein, and iron. It is high in beta-carotene (an immunity-boosting nutrient and precursor to vitamin A), which is fat-soluble. That means in order to get the maximum vitamin absorption from your sweet potato, you'll need some fat. Hallelujah! Whether you adorn your baked sweet potato with a pat of butter or pan-fry sweet potatoes in a little bacon grease, you can do so guilt-free!

You do not have to look far to find nutritionists singing the sweet potato's praises. In recent years, the sweet potato has become the darling of health columnists from coast to coast, a testament to the root's growing popularity outside of the South. Even carb-a-phobes relish the sweet potato as a "smart carb" due to its low glycemic index, or its neutral effect on blood sugar. Burger King, White Castle, and other national chains have added sweet potato fries and tots to their menus in recent years to meet the demand for healthier fast food. This market represents the biggest increase in sweet potato consumption.

Some research even suggests that the skin of the sweet potato can be used to produce a dietary supplement to control blood-glucose levels in diabetics. The Japanese have long used the skin of a white variety of sweet potato for this purpose, but recent research shows that the more common orange-skinned variety is just as effective.

Recently, the sweet potato has been viewed as an ideal crop for ending world hunger and disease due to its high nutritive value and ease of growth even in poor soils. It has steadily been replacing the true yam in Africa because it is considered a cure for childhood blindness associated with vitamin A deficiency.

Beyond its promise as a food crop, the sweet potato is currently being re-engineered by North Carolina State University scientists as a source of ethanol for the biofuel industry.

Reconnecting to Our Roots

Running counter to the trend of industrialization is a growing niche market for the sweet potato: the demand since the mid-1990s for heirlooms, or traditional, old-timey varieties. Heirlooms are less than ideal for commercial markets, in which sizes are graded, misshapen potatoes are culled, and high yields, appearance, and toleration of storage are everything. However, their superior flavor and storied histories make them prized by farmers' market shoppers and chefs alike.

In the farm-to-table local food movement, sweet potatoes are constants on restaurant menus and are being used creatively in countless artisan products from vodka to hot sauce. In North Carolina, Fullsteam Brewery makes a small-batch sweet potato lager named Carver, in honor of the great southern environmental scientist and sweet potato advocate, George Washington Carver. At Mississippi State University, students are reviving Carver's research endeavors in competition for a $2,500 cash prize for a new value-added product that would make use of Mississippi sweet potato seconds and culls.

Sweet Potatoes 101

VARIETIES

There are literally hundreds of varieties of sweet potatoes with a myriad of colors, textures, and tastes. The best way to explore them is to buy a couple of every variety you find, bake them slowly, and decide for yourself which ones you like. It is impossible to list them all, but here's a sampling of the varieties and types available in American markets.

Orange-fleshed "traditionals" This is what most people think of as a sweet potato—moist, orange-fleshed, and sweet. Regardless of how they are marketed, none of them are yams. There are subtle differences, most of them superficial or solely of concern to producers. All of these varieties are delicious. Greater variation results from growing and storage conditions than from variety. The most common commercial varieties are Beauregard, Covington, Jewel, and Garnet.

Sweet, moist whites and yellows The absence of beta-carotene means these varieties lack the characteristic carrot or pumpkin flavor of the orange sweet potato. Many heirlooms fall into this category, and I describe a few—Hayman and Nancy Hall—below. The only commercially grown white sweet potato found with any regularity in the South is the O'Henry. It is a white mutation of the Beauregard and was developed by Wayne Bailey of Cane Creek Farms in Vardaman, Mississippi. I am always proud to tell North Carolina farmers they are growing a Mississippi sweet potato! It can be used in any recipe that calls for an orange-fleshed variety, and it has similar sweetness and texture to the "traditionals."

Heirlooms An heirloom variety is simply a variety that has been passed down through generations. A huge amount of variation exists among heirlooms, and this is just a sampling of the ones I admire for their flavor and/or their story.

* *Hayman* It is said that this heirloom from Virginia's Eastern Shore is so delicious that the Devil would not have offered it to Eve; he would have eaten it himself. It is super sweet, pale inside and out, small, ugly, and prized by locals.
* *Nancy Hall* Out of the dozens of sweet potatoes she collects, conservation gardener Yanna Fishman nominated the Nancy Hall to Slow Food's Ark of Taste. It is an old-time North Carolina favorite with waxy, honey-flavored yellow flesh.
* *Violetta* A super sweet white-fleshed sweet potato with a pretty violet-purple skin. Excellent, very sweet flavor and one

of the most beautiful sweet potatoes to behold. A true sweet potato queen.

❋ *Mahon or Bradshaw* In a tasting of twelve varieties, this was my favorite. Light orange flesh with notes of butterscotch and brown sugar. The Mahon, unfortunately, was recently patented. The Bradshaw is a variety of the Mahon developed by a retired horticulture professor from Clemson, David Bradshaw.

Oriental or Japanese A few distinct types of Asian sweet potatoes are found in American markets. Japanese sweet potatoes have deep rosy skins that contrast beautifully with their ivory flesh. Their skins get wonderfully crisp when roasted, and their flavor is closer to that of chestnuts than the traditional orange sweet potato. There are also several purple-fleshed and -skinned varieties new to American markets. Most bear resemblance to the famous Okinawan purple sweet potatoes. All Purple is a traditional Japanese variety that lives up to its name—it is purple inside and out. A newly patented variety from North Carolina with a big marketing push in recent years is the Stokes Purple. Both are mildly sweet and have dry, mealy textures that can be bewildering to the uninitiated. The purple flesh reacts with baking powder in baking and turns an unappetizing gray. Ideal for savory applications, they crisp up beautifully due to their lower moisture content. The skin can be bitter, so you may wish to peel them.

HOW TO CHOOSE THEM

Buy sweet potatoes dirty by the bushel directly from a farmer if you can get them. They will be cheaper and keep much longer. Do not buy "fresh dug" or uncured sweet potatoes because the quality is inferior. Sweet potatoes should be cured in a warm, humid environment for a few weeks, a process that converts the starches to sugars, before they are sold. The harvest season is the end of summer, generally September and into October. They are cured and in their prime just in time for Thanksgiving. When stored properly, sweet potatoes will keep without deteriorating for up to a year. Size is generally not a determination of quality, though I have found that jumbo sweet potatoes have a tendency to be fibrous or "stringy." For best storage, choose sweet potatoes without any soft spots.

HOW TO STORE THEM

Unwashed sweet potatoes can keep for months in a cool, dark spot where the temperature does not dip below 55°. Once washed, sweet potatoes do not last more than a couple of weeks at room temperature. They should be stored in a well-ventilated area, such as a basket. Do not store them in the refrigerator, which creates hard white spots in the flesh and deteriorates the flavor and texture.

HOW TO PREPARE THEM

The most important thing to know about cooking sweet potatoes is that they should be cooked until they are completely soft in the center. Please, no al dente sweet potatoes! I regard the following methods as the most essential techniques for preparing sweet potatoes.

Mashing Many recipes in this collection call for mashed sweet potatoes or sweet potato purée. Start by baking or steaming the sweet potatoes, which produces the most flavorful mash and superior results in the recipes; I detail those methods below. Coarsely mash the warm, peeled sweet potatoes with a fork or potato masher or purée them in a food processor for a smoother texture. If your sweet potatoes seem particularly fibrous, you can pass them through a food mill or a fine-meshed sieve to remove the strings.

Steaming Steamed sweet potatoes have a luxurious, silky texture. Peeled and sliced or diced sweet potatoes steam quickly and hold their shape well. They can also be steamed whole, with or without the skins. Steam in a tightly covered pot on a rack over boiling water until completely tender when pierced with a sharp knife, 10–15 minutes for diced or 30–45 minutes for whole sweet potatoes. Steamed sweet potatoes are a mainstay in my refrigerator and are the basis for my favorite everyday breakfast. In a large cast-iron skillet, heat 1 tablespoon olive oil and a pinch of smoked paprika. Fry slices of steamed sweet potatoes for a few minutes on each side and top with a fried egg cooked in the same skillet.

Baking Slow-baked sweet potatoes have a rich, caramelized flavor. Wash the sweet potatoes well, then prick them all over with a fork. Place on a baking sheet lined with parchment paper or foil in a cold oven and bake at 350° until the flesh has collapsed away from the skins and the sugars have begun to seep, bubble, and burn on the baking sheet. The sweet potatoes will be completely soft when done, 1–1½ hours depending on the size. The skins will slip off easily while the sweet potatoes are still warm.

Frying Sweet potatoes can be fried as chips or French fries, but they need to be fried at a lower temperature than russet potatoes to avoid scorching. Soak thin slices or fries in ice water for an hour. Drain and pat completely dry. Deep-fry in small batches at 325° for 2 minutes for chips and 3 minutes for fries. Drain on brown paper bags. Raise the oil temperature to 350° and fry again until golden brown. Drain again on paper bags and salt generously.

Boiling Generally, I prefer to steam sweet potatoes instead of boiling them except in cases where the cooking water as well as the sweet potatoes will be utilized. You can, however, boil sweet potatoes whole with the skin on without the loss of flavor and nutrients. Place well-scrubbed sweet potatoes in the bottom of a heavy saucepan, cover with cold water, and add 1 teaspoon salt per pound of sweet potatoes. Cook until easily pierced with a sharp knife. Drain and cool slightly before slipping off the skins.

Microwaving Microwaving is one of the fastest ways to prepare sweet potatoes, but the results are inferior, lacking in sweetness and creaminess. Microwaving is, however, valuable as a time-saving partial cooking technique. Wash the sweet potatoes well, prick them all over with a fork, and microwave on high for 4–7 minutes, or until they give just slightly when squeezed with your fingertips. When cool enough to handle, cut into desired shapes and proceed with roasting, frying, sautéing, or grilling to finish.

The cooking time will be cut in half. Try adding par-microwaved sweet potatoes to your favorite kebobs. They absorb marinades particularly well.

Raw Sweet potatoes can be eaten raw. Cut into thin slices or batons and soak briefly in ice water for extra crunch. Serve with your favorite dip. They can also be grated raw in salads. Rinse to wash away the excess starch. Approach with caution: eating raw sweet potatoes can cause intestinal distress in some individuals. This fact has garnered them the nickname "poot-roots" from old-timers like my grandfather who ate countless raw sweet potatoes as a child while working in the fields.

MORE SWEET POTATO TIPS

* 1 medium sweet potato = ½ pound = approximately 1 cup mashed or chopped sweet potatoes
* To prevent cut sweet potatoes from turning brown, use a stainless steel knife (as opposed to carbon steel) and submerge them in cold water. This can be done days in advance of further preparation. Drain and blot dry with a clean towel before proceeding with your recipe.
* Bake more sweet potatoes than you need, then peel and freeze the extras in 2-cup portions to have on hand for recipes.
* Sweet potatoes are a beautiful addition to the home garden. My favorite source for slips is Southern Exposure Seed Exchange (www.southernexposure.com).
* In a sunny kitchen window, place a sweet potato in a quart jar of water and watch it grow. It will frame your window in beautiful vines in a couple of months, and the leaves are edible.

The Recipes

Limiting my selection of recipes to the fifty in this book was a challenge indeed—there are so many sweet potato possibilities. The recipes I have chosen are some of my favorite ways to showcase the sweet potato, and I hope you will try them all! When the variety is unspecified, the recipe was tested with traditional sweet and moist orange-fleshed sweet potatoes. Some recipes were developed for specific varieties, such as the chestnut-like, white-fleshed Japanese or O'Henry, and call for them by name.

The endless versatility of the sweet potato inspires creativity and a personal approach, and I have aimed to offer techniques to help you build your own repertoire. Regarding technique, perhaps the century-old *Picayune Creole Cook Book* says it best: preparing "the sweet potato is an art, for the delicate flavor of the potato is lost if it is not properly cooked." May you all be sweet potato artists!

Breakfast

MORNING PASTRIES, GRITS, GRAVY, AND HASH

The first sweet potato dish I became known for was my sweet potato biscuits. I still find the golden hue and soft texture of sweet potato–enriched breads irresistible. At my stand at the Carrboro Farmers' Market, my best-selling morning pastries are Sweet Potato–Ginger Scones and Sunshine Buns, both of which have mashed roasted sweet potatoes in the dough. While it is true that sweet potatoes turn everyday breads into something spectacular, the genius was born out of necessity. Enslaved Africans used sweet potatoes to extend their meager flour rations. Years later, George Washington Carver helped save U.S. soldiers from a wheat shortage during World War I by adding sweet potatoes to the bread dough, which not only reduced the amount of flour needed but also made the bread more nutritious.

The sweet potato is a natural at the breakfast table in other forms as well. Whether replacing regular old potatoes or stirred into grits, sweet potatoes provide an easy way to start the day with a healthy helping of vitamin-packed vegetables!

Sweet Potato Doughnut Muffins

Somewhere between the cupcake craze and the doughnut craze, doughnut muffins began showing up everywhere. If you love doughnuts but would never attempt making them at home, this recipe is for you. Who can resist the taste of a doughnut in an easy-to-prepare muffin? The addition of sweet potatoes makes for a tender crumb and creates perfect harmony with the spiced-sugar coating. Your family will love you for these!

MAKES 1 DOZEN STANDARD MUFFINS

OR 2 DOZEN MINI-MUFFINS

FOR THE MUFFINS

3 cups sifted unbleached all-purpose flour

2 teaspoons baking powder

1/2 teaspoon baking soda

1 teaspoon kosher salt

1/2 teaspoon freshly grated nutmeg

1/2 cup buttermilk

1 tablespoon finely grated orange zest

1 1/4 cup mashed sweet potatoes (page 14)

1 stick unsalted butter, at room temperature

3/4 cup sugar

2 large eggs

FOR THE SPICED-SUGAR COATING

1 stick melted unsalted butter

1 cup sugar

2 teaspoons cinnamon

1/2 teaspoon ginger

1/2 teaspoon allspice

Preheat the oven to 350°. Butter and flour a 12-cup muffin tin or 24-cup mini-muffin tin.

In a small bowl, whisk together the flour, baking powder, baking soda, salt, and nutmeg. In another small bowl, whisk together the buttermilk, orange zest, and mashed sweet potatoes.

In the bowl of a stand mixer, cream the butter and sugar together until light and fluffy. Beat in the eggs one at a time until fully incorporated. Gently stir in the flour mixture, alternating with the sweet potato mixture until just combined. Do not overmix.

Spoon the batter into the muffin cups and bake for about 30 minutes or until a cake tester comes out clean.

While the muffins are baking, prepare the spiced-sugar coating. Place the melted butter in a medium bowl. In a separate bowl, stir together the sugar and spices.

When the muffins are done, place the muffin tin on a wire rack until cool enough to handle (about 10 minutes), then remove the muffins. Brush them all over with melted butter, then roll in the spiced-sugar mixture. Place on a wire rack to cool. Serve warm or at room temperature.

These muffins are best the day they are made, but they also freeze perfectly for up to 3 months..

Sweet Potato–Sour Cream Coffee Cake

If you have weekend houseguests, this is the cake you want on your pedestal. It is a fuss-free keeper and sublime with a cup of coffee. Even the best coffee cake can be improved by the addition of sweet potatoes, which offer additional moisture and a gorgeous autumnal color.

MAKES 8–10 SERVINGS

FOR THE TOPPING

1/4 cup all-purpose flour

1/4 cup brown sugar

1 1/2 teaspoons cinnamon

2 tablespoons cold unsalted butter, cut into small pieces

1 cup chopped pecans

FOR THE COFFEE CAKE

2 cups sifted cake flour

1/2 teaspoon freshly grated nutmeg

1 1/2 teaspoons baking powder

1/2 teaspoon baking soda

1/2 teaspoon kosher salt

2 sticks unsalted butter, at room temperature

2 cups sugar

4 large eggs, at room temperature

1 cup sour cream

1 1/2 cups mashed sweet potatoes (page 14)

1 teaspoon vanilla

Preheat the oven to 350°. Butter and flour a 10-inch tube pan.

To make the topping, in a small bowl, combine the flour, brown sugar, and cinnamon with your hands. Pinch in the butter until the mixture is crumbly, then mix in the pecans.

To make the coffee cake, sift together the flour, nutmeg, baking powder, baking soda, and salt. In the bowl of a stand mixer, cream the butter and sugar together until light and fluffy. Beat in the eggs one at a time until well blended. Turn the mixer on high and beat 1 minute. With the mixer on low speed, alternately add the flour mixture and the sour cream. Then gently fold in the mashed sweet potatoes and vanilla until well blended.

Pour three-quarters of the cake batter into the prepared tube pan. Top with three-quarters of the streusel, then add the remaining cake batter and sprinkle the remaining streusel on top.

Bake 50–60 minutes or until a cake tester comes out clean. Cool in the pan on a wire rack for 15 minutes, then remove from the pan and place on the rack to cool completely. Transfer to a cake stand or serving platter, streusel side up, and top with powdered sugar or a simple glaze if you like.

Sweet Potato–Bran Muffins

Can we admit that most muffins are just cake that is acceptable to eat for breakfast? As the mother and wife of two of the world's most devoted muffin-lovers, I sought to create a muffin I could feel good about serving my family. This one is packed with fiber and just sweet enough to satisfy. To make them even more healthful, I use virgin coconut oil, which adds the intoxicating scent of toasted coconut. Feel free to substitute another vegetable oil or melted butter if you prefer.

MAKES 1 DOZEN

2 cups oat bran

$\frac{1}{2}$ cup unbleached all-purpose flour

1 teaspoon baking powder

1 teaspoon baking soda

$\frac{3}{4}$ teaspoon kosher salt

1 teaspoon allspice

$\frac{3}{4}$ cup buttermilk

$\frac{1}{2}$ cup melted virgin coconut oil

$\frac{1}{2}$ cup maple syrup

1 tablespoon finely grated orange zest, packed

2 large eggs

1 cup peeled and grated sweet potatoes, packed

$\frac{1}{2}$ cup raisins

$\frac{1}{2}$ cup chopped toasted walnuts

Preheat the oven to 300°.

Spread the oat bran on a baking sheet and toast for 10 minutes, stirring halfway through to prevent it from burning around the edges. Remove from the oven and cool.

Increase the oven temperature to 350°.

Line a 12-cup muffin tin with paper baking liners. Lightly butter the top of the muffin tin so the muffins will not stick as they puff up over the tops.

In a large bowl, whisk together the flour, baking powder, baking soda, salt, and allspice.

In a medium bowl, whisk together the buttermilk, oil, maple syrup, orange zest, and eggs until well combined.

When the bran has cooled, stir it into the flour mixture, then whisk in the wet ingredients until just combined. Fold in the grated sweet potatoes, raisins, and walnuts.

Divide the batter among the muffin cups, filling them quite full and mounding them slightly for a beautiful domed-top muffin. Bake for about 30 minutes or until a cake tester comes out clean. Cool on a wire rack for 10 minutes, then remove the muffins from the cups. Serve warm or at room temperature.

Sweet Potato Biscuits with Chorizo Gravy

I am a biscuit disciple. Every year I visit my friend Kelly Alexander's food-writing class at Duke University to demonstrate proper biscuit making to the uninitiated. The fact is that even the most detailed description of biscuit making is a poor replacement for observation.

Most recipes call for biscuit dough to be kneaded, a technique of folding and compressing that develops gluten and creates a sturdy structure in yeasted bread dough. But kneading is exactly what you should avoid when making biscuits. While the motion of gathering biscuit dough by pulling and pushing is similar to kneading, it lacks all of the vigor. In the words of the late Bill Neal, "Biscuits, like all baking but more so, are in the hands, not the head."

That said, we have to start somewhere. Everyone can agree on a few elements required for success: soft southern flour, buttermilk, very cold ingredients, a gentle touch, and a hot oven. In this recipe, the addition of sweet potatoes makes a softer biscuit with delicate sweetness and an elegant apricot hue. That sweetness provides the perfect foil for slivers of salt-kissed country ham, the ultimate southern cocktail nibble. Sausage gravy made with lip-tingling, Mexican-style chorizo, however, is destined to become a new classic. If you do not want to make your own, chorizo is readily available, given the recent wave of Mexican immigrants to the southeastern United States. This is particularly true in sweet potato country, where the largely Hispanic migrant labor force is indispensable to the hand-harvested crop. Be sure to buy soft, fresh chorizo, not hard, aged Spanish-style chorizo.

FOR THE CHORIZO

1 pound ground pork

2 teaspoons kosher salt

2 small garlic cloves, finely minced

$1\frac{1}{2}$ tablespoons New Mexican or Guajillo chili powder

$\frac{1}{2}$ teaspoon cayenne

$\frac{1}{2}$ teaspoon cumin

$\frac{1}{2}$ teaspoon Mexican oregano

Pinch of cinnamon

$\frac{1}{2}$ teaspoon freshly ground black pepper

2 tablespoons cider vinegar

FOR THE BISCUITS

5 cups sifted unbleached pastry flour or all-purpose flour

1 tablespoon plus 1 teaspoon baking powder

$\frac{1}{8}$ teaspoon freshly grated nutmeg

1 tablespoon kosher salt

1 teaspoon finely grated lemon zest, packed

2 sticks very cold unsalted butter, cut into 1-inch pieces

1 cup cold buttermilk

$1\frac{1}{2}$ cups cold mashed sweet potatoes (page 14)

1 tablespoon sorghum molasses or brown sugar

2 tablespoons melted salted butter

FOR THE CHORIZO GRAVY

1 pound chorizo sausage

2 tablespoons sifted all-purpose flour

$2\frac{1}{2}$ cups whole milk

2 tablespoons sour cream

2 tablespoons chopped cilantro

Preheat the oven to 500°.

To make the chorizo, combine all ingredients well in a medium bowl. Cover with plastic wrap and let marinade in the refrigerator overnight or at least 2 hours.

To make the biscuits, in a large bowl whisk together the flour, baking powder, nutmeg, salt, and lemon zest. Cut the butter into the flour mixture in a food processor, with a pastry blender, or with cold fingers until it is the size of corn kernels.

In a medium bowl, mix together the buttermilk, mashed sweet potatoes, and sorghum molasses or brown sugar. Stir the buttermilk mixture into the flour mixture to make a soft, slightly sticky dough. Be careful not to overwork the dough.

Gather the dough on a floured surface and with floured hands press it out into a rectangle about 1 inch thick. Fold the dough in half, make a quarter turn, then press it out again. Repeat this process one more time, ending up with a rectangle a generous ¾ inch thick. (This process of folding the dough creates beautiful flaky layers.)

Flour a 3-inch biscuit cutter and cut out the biscuits, taking care not to twist as you cut. Use a bench scraper or spatula to transfer the biscuits to a baking sheet lined with parchment paper, leaving about 1 fingertip of space between them. Brush the tops with melted butter.

Bake for 12–15 minutes or until deep golden brown. Check after 10 minutes and rotate the pan for even baking.

To make the chorizo gravy, brown the sausage in a large, heavy skillet over medium-high heat. Sprinkle with the flour and cook, stirring constantly until the flour is brown and toasty. Whisk in the milk and bring to a low boil. Simmer until thick, about 5 minutes. Stir in the sour cream, spoon over split biscuits, and garnish with cilantro.

VARIATION ❋ Sweet Potato–Cheddar Biscuits: Omit the nutmeg, lemon zest, and sorghum molasses. Reduce the unsalted butter to 1 stick. Add ½ teaspoon cayenne to the dry ingredients. Stir in 1 cup grated sharp cheddar after you cut the butter into the flour.

Sunshine Buns

After my son was born in 2010, midnight baking sessions for the Saturday morning farmers' market became impossible. Years later, I still have customers come by every Saturday morning to ask when these Sunshine Buns will be back. They are a sweet potato and cardamom twist on the cinnamon roll or sticky bun. Take it from my customers: they are swoon-worthy, and now you can make your own at home. A superb recipe for yeasted sweet potato bread forms the base of these rolls and can be adapted to a number of recipes. It makes 2 loaves of wonderful, soft sandwich bread (try it with curried chicken salad) that is also delicious toasted. You can turn the dough into monkey bread, which I include as a variation below.

MAKES ABOUT 1 DOZEN

FOR THE DOUGH

1 pound sweet potatoes, peeled and sliced ½ inch thick

2 cups water

1 tablespoon kosher salt

6 tablespoons unsalted butter

3 large eggs, beaten

¾ cup milk or buttermilk

1 tablespoon active dry yeast

3 tablespoons sugar or honey

5–6 cups unbleached all-purpose flour

FOR THE FILLING

1½ cups brown sugar

4 teaspoons cardamom

4 teaspoons cinnamon

¼ cup unbleached all-purpose flour

10 tablespoons unsalted butter, at room temperature

Pinch of kosher salt

Place the sweet potatoes in a heavy saucepan with the water and add the salt. Cover and bring to a boil. Simmer over medium-high heat for about 20 minutes until tender, then remove the lid and cook off any remaining liquid. Stir in the butter. Let cool slightly, then stir in the eggs. Cool to lukewarm or about 105°.

Meanwhile, bring the milk or buttermilk to a low boil and remove from heat. Cool to lukewarm. If you use buttermilk, it will curdle, but that is fine.

In a large bowl, whisk the yeast and sugar or honey into the lukewarm milk. When the sweet potato mixture has cooled, stir it into the yeast and then begin stirring in the flour with a wooden spoon. Knead on a well-floured board, adding flour as necessary, until the dough is satiny and not too sticky to handle (a slightly sticky dough performs well if you are comfortable handling it). Knead by hand for 10–15 minutes or for 5–7 minutes in a stand mixer.

Place the dough in a large greased bowl. Cover with a towel and let rise until doubled in bulk—about 1½ hours at room temperature or overnight in the refrigerator. If you refrigerate the dough, allow an hour or more for it to reach room temperature before proceeding with the recipe.

Using your hands or a wooden spoon, mix the filling ingredients together in a medium bowl.

Generously butter a 12-cup muffin tin, including the top of the pan to prevent the buns from sticking when they rise over the tops.

When the dough has risen, punch it down and transfer it to a well-floured surface. Roll it out into a 24 × 16-inch rectangle. Spread the filling evenly on the dough all the way to the edges. Beginning on one long side, roll it up jelly-roll style and cut it crosswise into 12 pieces. Place one bun in each muffin cup. Cover loosely with plastic wrap and let rise at room temperature until very puffy, about 1 hour.

Preheat the oven to 400°.

After the buns have risen, place the muffin tin on a rimmed baking sheet lined with parchment paper to catch any drips. Bake until golden brown and cooked through, about 25 minutes. Use a sharp paring knife or cake tester to check that a bun in the center of the tin is no longer doughy. Let cool in the pan on a wire rack for 5 minutes before inverting the buns onto a large serving platter or another pan lined with parchment paper. Drizzle any goo that remains in the muffin tins over the buns. Serve warm or at room temperature. These are best eaten the day they are made.

VARIATIONS ❋ Sweet Potato–Cardamom Monkey Bread: Preheat the oven to 350° and butter 1 tube pan or 2 loaf pans. Omit the filling. Melt 4 tablespoons unsalted butter and place in a small bowl. Combine 1/2 cup sugar with 1/2 teaspoon each of cardamom and cinnamon in another bowl. Pinch off walnut-sized pieces of the dough, dip them in the butter, roll them in the spiced sugar (or sprinkle them with the sugar if you prefer them less sweet), and layer them in the pan. Cover the dough with plastic wrap and let rise until very puffy, about 1 hour. Bake until the loaf is firm and deep golden brown on top and no longer doughy in the center, about 45 minutes. Let cool slightly on a wire rack, then remove from the pan. Serve warm or at room temperature, encouraging guests to pinch off bites of the bread with their hands.

Sweet Potato Yeast Bread: Preheat the oven to 375° and butter 2 loaf pans. Omit the filling. Divide the dough evenly between the pans, cover loosely with plastic wrap, and let rise at room temperature for about 1 hour. Brush with an egg wash and bake for 50–60 minutes until deep golden brown and done in the center.

Yeasted Sweet Potato Waffles

Sweet potato pancake recipes abound and are worthy of explora-
tion. These yeasted sweet potato waffles, however, are in a league of
their own. Do not be intimidated by the addition of yeast. Quickly
mixed the night before and left to rise while you sleep, they are vir-
tually effortless. Have them for breakfast, for dessert topped with
sweet potato ice cream, or for dinner with fried chicken. For added
crunch, I sprinkle the batter with spiced turbinado sugar when I
spoon it into the waffle iron. If you omit this step, you could add
another tablespoon of sugar and a pinch of cinnamon to the batter
to compensate.

MAKES ABOUT 8

- 2 cups unbleached all-purpose flour
- 1 tablespoon brown sugar
- 1 teaspoon instant yeast
- 1¼ teaspoons kosher salt
- ½ teaspoon freshly grated nutmeg
- 1½ teaspoons cinnamon, divided
- 1 teaspoon finely grated lemon zest
- 1 stick melted unsalted butter
- 1 cup mashed sweet potatoes (page 14),
    warm or at room temperature
- 1¼ cups warm milk
- ½ cup turbinado sugar
- 1½ teaspoons vanilla
- 2 large eggs, beaten
- ¼ teaspoon baking soda

In a large bowl (with plenty of room for the batter to rise), whisk together the flour, the brown sugar, the yeast, the salt, the nutmeg, ½ teaspoon of the cinnamon, and the lemon zest. Stir in the melted butter, being sure that it is no hotter than 110° or it will kill the yeast. In a small bowl, whisk together the mashed sweet potatoes and milk and stir them into the flour mixture until well combined. Cover the top of the bowl tightly with plastic wrap and leave on the counter overnight or at least 12 hours.

After the batter has risen, preheat a waffle iron. Stir together the turbinado sugar and the remaining 1 teaspoon of cinnamon in a small bowl. Stir the vanilla, eggs, and baking soda into the batter.

Spray the waffle iron lightly with nonstick spray (even if your iron is already nonstick). Sprinkle the bottom of the waffle iron with cinnamon sugar and spoon the batter on top (about ½–¾ cup for a standard waffle iron). The batter should be thick and should not run to the edges. Use an icing spatula or the back of a spoon to spread the batter, leaving about a 1-inch border all around. Sprinkle the top with more cinnamon sugar and close the waffle maker. Bake until good and brown for crispy waffles, generally a few minutes longer than the waffle maker says. The waffle will be quite dark due to the caramelized cinnamon sugar. You may have to make a test waffle before you find the sweet spot!

Remove the waffle, spray the iron again, and repeat with the remaining batter. You can keep the waffles warm in the oven until you make the entire batch or serve them straight away with good butter and warm maple syrup or fried chicken and honey.

Sweet Potato–Ginger Scones

During five years of peddling scones at the Saturday morning Carrboro Farmers' Market, this variation was far and away the best-seller. Craggy on the outside, fluffy on the inside, and studded with chunks of pungent ginger, these scones are feasts for the senses. The amount of liquid needed in this recipe varies depending on the amount of moisture in your sweet potatoes. Overly wet dough will not spoil your efforts, but it will make your scones spread more and be softer rather than crisp on the outside. You want the dough to just hold together. Also, for the best results, be sure that the mashed sweet potatoes are well chilled before adding them to the dough, or the butter will melt and damage the texture of the scones.

MAKES ABOUT 1 DOZEN

FOR THE SCONES

1/4 cup cold heavy cream

3/4 cup cold buttermilk

1 1/2 cups cold mashed sweet potatoes (page 14)

5 cups unbleached pastry flour or all-purpose flour

1 tablespoon plus 1 teaspoon baking powder

1 teaspoon kosher salt

2/3 cup sugar

1/2 teaspoon cardamom

1/8 teaspoon freshly grated nutmeg

3 sticks very cold unsalted butter, cut into 1-inch pieces

2 teaspoons lemon zest

1/2 cup chopped crystallized ginger

FOR THE TOPPING

1/4 cup cream

1/4 cup turbinado sugar

1/8 teaspoon cardamom

Preheat the oven to 400°. Line a baking sheet with parchment paper.

In a small bowl, whisk the cream and buttermilk into the mashed sweet potatoes.

In a large bowl, sift together the flour, baking powder, salt, sugar, cardamom, and nutmeg. Cut the butter into the flour mixture with a pastry blender or a fork until it is the size of corn kernels. Stir in the lemon zest and crystallized ginger.

Make a well in the center of the flour mixture and, working quickly, stir in the sweet potato mixture until the dough just comes together. Using your hands or a wooden spoon, drop the dough onto the baking sheet into mounds about 2½ inches in diameter and about 2 inches apart.

For the topping, brush the scones with the cream. Mix the turbinado sugar and cardamom in a small bowl and sprinkle it evenly over the top of each scone. Bake for about 30 minutes or until golden brown. Serve warm or at room temperature.

Virginia Willis's Sweet Potato Grits

The first time I laid eyes on this recipe, I was skeptical. Sometimes it seems like folks should just leave grits alone. But I trust Virginia Willis's taste, and she did not disappoint. This recipe works. It yields the creamiest grits with a gorgeous autumnal hue and just a touch of sweetness, which bring out the best in a side of greens or country ham with red-eye gravy.

MAKES 4–6 SERVINGS

2 cups water

2 cups lowfat or whole milk

1 cup stone-ground grits

2 medium sweet potatoes (about 1 pound), peeled and grated

Kosher salt and freshly ground white pepper

¼ teaspoon ginger

Pinch of cinnamon

1 tablespoon unsalted butter

In a large, heavy saucepan, combine the water and milk and bring to a gentle boil over medium-high heat. Slowly add the grits, whisking constantly, then add the grated sweet potatoes. Season with salt and white pepper. Decrease heat to low and simmer, stirring often, until the grits are creamy and thick, 45–60 minutes.

Taste the grits to make sure the grits and sweet potato are both tender. Add the ginger, cinnamon, and butter. Taste and adjust for seasoning with salt and white pepper. Serve immediately.

VARIATION ✻ Sweet Potato Spoonbread: Preheat the oven to 375°. Butter an ovenproof casserole dish or round 2-quart soufflé mold. To the sweet potato grits, add 2 large egg yolks, one at a time, stirring after each addition. In a separate bowl, using a handheld mixer, beat 2 large egg whites with a pinch of salt on high speed until stiff peaks form. Gently fold the egg whites into the warm sweet potato grits mixture. Transfer the grits to the prepared pan and smooth the surface with a spatula. Bake until the outside is puffed and raised, the inside is firm but moist, and the top is golden brown, 35–40 minutes. Serve immediately while still puffed.

Sweet Potato, Bacon, and Apple Hash

Topped with a fried egg, this might be my ideal breakfast. It is the perfect fuel before a weekend hike. Use the best thick-cut, hardwood-smoked bacon you can find for this recipe. A particularly smoky bacon like Benton's shines alongside the gentle sweetness of this dish, and apples with a bit of tartness really bring the flavors together. This recipe works well with traditional orange sweet potatoes, but it is also a great cooking method for the drier, starchier varieties like Stokes Purple or Japanese. You can opt to leave the skins on for a fiber boost.

MAKES 6 SERVINGS

6 ounces thick-cut bacon, cut into $1/2$-inch dice

4 cups peeled, diced sweet potatoes

2 cups chopped onions

1 bay leaf

1 teaspoon kosher salt

$1/2$ cup chopped red bell peppers

2 cups chopped Golden Delicious, Granny Smith,
   or other tart cooking apples

Pinch of cayenne

Freshly ground black pepper

2 tablespoons chopped parsley or handful of arugula

In a large cast-iron skillet, sauté the bacon until crisp. Transfer with a slotted spoon to a plate and pour off all but 3 tablespoons of the drippings.

Add the sweet potatoes, onions, bay leaf, and salt to the skillet. Cover and cook over medium heat for 8–10 minutes, stirring every minute or so. Scrape the bottom of the pan often so the hash does not burn. When the sweet potatoes are just tender, add the peppers, apples, and cayenne. Continue to cook over medium heat until the peppers and apples are tender, about 5 minutes more.

Remove the bay leaf. Stir in the reserved bacon. Season with pepper and more salt if needed. Sprinkle with the chopped parsley or toss in a handful of arugula. Serve straight from the skillet, preferably with fried or poached eggs on top.

Sweet Potato–Sour Cherry Butter

Too often sweet potato butter tastes like cloyingly sweet mashed sweet potatoes. This recipe is my attempt to redeem it. The tart cherries provide acidity and depth, while the vanilla and cardamom offer a nice aromatic change from the expected cinnamon. This butter was one of a few southern preserves featured in the Preserves Pavilion at Slow Food Nation in 2008. It is delicious on biscuits, of course, but try it swirled into your oatmeal or as a filling for tarts or fried pies.

MAKES ABOUT 8 CUPS

4 medium sweet potatoes (about 2 pounds),
   peeled and sliced 1 inch thick
8 ounces dried sour cherries (or 1 pound fresh)
1 (12-ounce) bottle of spicy ginger ale, preferably Blenheim's
1½ cups water
½ teaspoon kosher salt
Seeds and pulp from 1 vanilla bean
2 teaspoons cardamom
Finely grated zest of 1 lemon
2 cups sugar
⅓ cup lemon juice

In a large, heavy saucepan, combine the sweet potatoes, cherries, ginger ale, water, and salt. Add the seeds from the vanilla bean to the saucepan along with the cardamom and lemon zest. Cover tightly and cook until the sweet potatoes are falling-apart tender. Add more water if needed to keep the sweet potatoes from burning.

Purée in a food processor or with an immersion blender. Over medium heat, stir in the sugar until dissolved, then stir in the lemon juice.

This butter can be stored in sterilized containers in the refrigerator for 1 month or can be frozen for up to 1 year. The National Center for Food Preservation advises against home canning of sweet potato butter.

Sides and Salads

VINTAGE CLASSICS AND
FRESH, MODERN TWISTS

I hope these recipes illustrate the versatility of sweet potatoes and convince you that they deserve more than a seasonal tribute on the Thanksgiving table. I have made every effort to include a variety of recipes that place equal value on tradition, technique, and novelty. Traditional recipes are often shunned because our opinions of them are based on uninspired institutional adaptations. I seek to rectify those misconceptions with stunning versions of sweet potato casserole, candied sweet potatoes, and sweet potato pone. At the same time, I offer fresh and exciting new sides to eat your way through as well.

Sweet Potatoes Baked in Ashes with Rosemary Butter

The most exquisite sweet potatoes I have ever eaten were served to me by an Israeli-born, New Orleans–residing, Philadelphia-raised chef at breakfast on the final day of the 2011 Southern Foodways Alliance symposium in Oxford, Mississippi. Ash-baked sweet potatoes were common fare in the hearth cooking of yesteryear, but these were the first I had ever tasted. They are a signature dish of Alon Shaya, who regularly roasts heirloom sweet potatoes in the embers and ashes of his pecan wood–fired pizza oven at New Orleans's Domenica and serves them painted with Louisiana cane syrup. Shaya clearly has absorbed the culture of his adopted home because these sweet potatoes are steeped in Louisiana pride. I have attempted to re-create the dish here. No sweet potatoes are more delicious, but consider yourself warned: these are not the sweet potatoes you want to serve at a high society affair. They are beautifully rustic and will stain your fingertips black.

MAKES 4 SERVINGS

4 medium sweet potatoes (about 2 pounds), unpeeled and scrubbed

Good-sized hardwood fire burned down to ashes in a grill, fireplace, or pizza oven, plus another pile of glowing embers

Long-handled tongs

Brush and/or soft towel to clean the cooked sweet potatoes

Rosemary butter

Pierce each sweet potato several times with a fork. Bury the sweet potatoes in a pile of hot ashes and cover with hot embers. After 30 minutes, remove 1 sweet potato with the tongs and test it. It should be completely soft in the center. You can add additional embers to the top of the pile if the sweet potatoes appear to be cooking too slowly. When completely tender, remove all the sweet potatoes and rub with a soft towel to remove as much ash as possible.

To make the rosemary butter, in a small saucepan melt a stick or two of best-quality salted butter and add a couple of short sprigs of rosemary. Simmer very slowly for about 5 minutes. Remove the rosemary sprigs and spoon the butter over hot, split sweet potatoes. You can also serve the sweet potatoes with warm cane syrup or sorghum molasses, salt, and pepper.

Perfect Baked "Jacket" Sweet Potatoes

Louisiana Cajuns call their sweet potatoes bon bon du close, *or "candy from the field." One taste of slow-baked, properly cured sweet potatoes, and you will understand why. If you do not have a convenient pile of hot ashes in which to bury your sweet potatoes, oven baking is fine. Traditional orange sweet potatoes will seep sugars that bubble and caramelize on the baking sheet. This is perfection! The caramelized sugars offer a touch of bitterness to balance the sweetness and give incredible depth of flavor to such a simple, honest food. All sweet potatoes, but particularly the drier-fleshed varieties, benefit from starting in a cold oven and baking at a lower temperature. This allows more time for the starch in the sweet potatoes to be converted to sugar, which happens between 135° and 175°. I always bake an ovenful and then stock the freezer with mashed sweet potatoes for use in other recipes down the road. Greasing the skins is certainly not necessary, but if you lightly rub bacon grease on the skins, then dust them with flaky sea salt, I promise you there will be no skins left on your diners' plates. You can serve your spuds simply, or you can get creative with some of the variations offered below.*

MAKES 4 SERVINGS

---

4 medium sweet potatoes (about 2 pounds), unpeeled and scrubbed

Bacon grease, unsalted butter, or olive oil (optional)

Maldon sea salt and freshly ground black pepper (optional)

Unsalted butter or topping of your choice

Prick the sweet potatoes all over with a fork. If desired, rub all over with the fat of your choice and sprinkle with sea salt and pepper. Place on a baking sheet lined with parchment paper or foil in a cold oven and bake at 350° until the flesh has collapsed away from the skins and the sweet potatoes are completely soft, 1–1½ hours depending on the size of the sweet potatoes.

Split and season with butter, salt, and pepper or add the topping of your choice. Alternately, peel and mash the sweet potatoes when cool enough to handle and use in your favorite recipe.

TOP-NOTCH TOPPINGS ❋ Chili-lime butter: Combine 2 tablespoons lime juice, 1 split hot chili pepper, 1 tablespoon brown sugar, and 4 tablespoons unsalted butter in a bowl and microwave for 1 minute. Discard the pepper and drizzle the butter over the sweet potatoes. Season with salt and pepper and sprinkle with chopped cilantro.

Sautéed pears, blue or goat cheese, and chopped walnuts: Sauté thinly sliced pears in unsalted butter with a pinch of kosher salt until soft. Spoon over the sweet potatoes and top with cheese crumbles, walnuts, a drizzle of honey, and a pinch of cayenne.

Brown sugar–Dijon butter (inspired by Raleigh, North Carolina, chef Ashley Christensen's Beasley's Chicken and Honey): Stir together 2 tablespoons brown sugar, 1 tablespoon Dijon mustard, 4 tablespoons soft unsalted butter, and a pinch of kosher salt.

Curry butter: Stir 1 teaspoon fresh, aromatic curry powder into 4 tablespoons soft unsalted butter.

Other good stuff: Sautéed mushrooms, garlicky greens, New Orleans–style barbecued shrimp, chili, or beans.

Mashed Sweet Potatoes with Spiced Brown Butter

Mashed sweet potatoes are the beloved first food of many, my son included. In their simplest form, they are added to dozens of recipes in this book and beyond.

Topping mashed sweet potatoes with spiced brown butter turns them from simple to spectacular. The butter provides a warm base note and a pleasant bitterness that balances the sweetness and creates a surprisingly rich and full flavor without a drop of added sugar.

Sweet potatoes are also wonderful mashed with other root vegetables, like rutabagas, which I have included as a variation. Though I love rutabagas straight, many find their turnip-y flavor overwhelming and their watery texture off the mark. Sweet potatoes to the rescue! The sweet potato's sweetness and creaminess perfectly balance the rough-around-the-edges rutabaga, while the rutabaga points the sweet potato in a decidedly savory direction. My friend Bill Smith tops Crook's Corner's mashed rutabagas with garlic butter, and I follow his wisdom here.

I always use either baked or steamed sweet potatoes for mash and include instructions for both methods here. Baking produces the most concentrated flavor and sweetness, while steaming creates a silkier purée and takes less time.

MAKES 6–8 SERVINGS

6 medium sweet potatoes (about 3 pounds),
    unpeeled and scrubbed
1 stick unsalted butter
Small handful of sage leaves or rosemary sprig
1 cinnamon stick
2 cloves
½ cup cream
Kosher salt and freshly ground black pepper

Cook the sweet potatoes by steaming or baking. To steam, peel the sweet potatoes and cut them into chunks or slices. Steam in a tightly covered pot on a rack over boiling water until completely tender when pierced with a sharp knife, 15–20 minutes. They can also be steamed whole with the peel on. Increase the time accordingly and slip off the skins when cool enough to handle.

To bake, prick the sweet potatoes all over with a fork. Place on a baking sheet lined with parchment paper or foil in a cold oven and bake at 350° until the flesh has collapsed away from the skins and the sweet potatoes are completely soft, 1–1½ hours depending on the size of the sweet potatoes. When cool enough to handle, slip off the skins.

To make the brown butter, in a small saucepan, melt the butter over medium heat. Throw in the sage or rosemary and spices. Continue to cook until the butter foams, the foam subsides, and the butter begins to darken. Swirl the pan from time to time to ensure even cooking. When the butter smells toasty and nutty, it is ready. Remove from heat and strain through a fine-meshed sieve.

Warm the cream in a small saucepan. Do not boil.

While still hot, purée the sweet potatoes with the cream in a food processor until smooth. Alternately, press the sweet potatoes through a fine-meshed sieve, process in a food mill, or mash with a potato masher, then whisk in the cream. Mix in all but a tablespoon of the brown butter mixture and season with salt and pepper to taste. Drizzle with the remaining butter.

VARIATION ❋ Garlic Butter Sweets and Rutabagas: Replace half the sweet potatoes with peeled and chunked rutabagas (or parsnips) and steam the sweet potatoes and rutabagas. Large and unwieldy rutabagas can be steamed whole until slightly softened before peeling. Mash or purée with the cream. Omit the spiced brown butter and top with unsalted butter that has been simmered with a generous tablespoon of chopped garlic until it is just golden. Be careful not to burn the garlic. Season well with salt and pepper.

OTHER TIPS ✳ Beyond their role as a side dish, Mashed Sweet Potatoes with Spiced Brown Butter can serve as the base for many other dishes:
— Use as a filling for ravioli.
— Thin with broth for soup.
— Chill and form into balls around marshmallows. Roll in crushed cornflakes and fry at 350° until golden brown. Alternately, brush all over with unsalted butter and bake at 400° until golden brown. Kids love these retro treats.
— Sweeten to taste and beat in a couple of eggs for pie filling or a baked pudding or casserole. You'll need about $2\frac{1}{2}$ cups mashed sweet potatoes, 2 eggs, and $\frac{3}{4}$ cups of sugar per pie.
— For a savory pie or tart filling, beat a couple of eggs and $\frac{1}{2}$ cup grated Parmesan or Pecorino Romano into $2\frac{1}{2}$ cups mashed sweet potatoes.

Candied Sweet Potatoes

The genius of southern food is less in its individual dishes than in the overall composition of the meal. Syrupy sweet potatoes balance earthy field peas and sharp turnip greens shot through with hot pepper vinegar. Crispy cornbread swoops in to sop it all up. Here is a particularly nuanced version of ubiquitous candied sweet potatoes that makes use of that coffee can of bacon grease my grandparents and parents kept above the stove.

MAKES 6 SERVINGS

---

4 medium sweet potatoes (about 2 pounds),
    peeled and sliced ½ inch thick
3 tablespoons unsalted butter
1 tablespoon bacon drippings
1 cup sugar
¾ teaspoon kosher salt
⅓ cup water
1 tablespoon lemon juice

Layer the sweet potatoes in a large cast-iron skillet. Dot with the butter and bacon drippings, and sprinkle with the sugar and salt. Pour the water and lemon juice over the sweet potatoes and cover the skillet with a tight-fitting lid or foil. Simmer for 15 minutes. Remove the cover and simmer until the sweet potatoes are very tender and the sauce is thick, 30–35 minutes more. Baste the sweet potatoes with the syrup from time to time, being careful not to break them up.

Sweet Potato Pone

Hundreds of versions of this grated sweet potato pudding or pone can be found in historical and community cookbooks. Creole variations often contain a generous shot of black pepper, which I have come to love. Well-heeled versions might call for orange blossom or rose water. With equal depth and breadth, sweet potato pone is the sixth man of traditional southern cuisine. It is often served as a side dish to pork or game but is also right at home with afternoon coffee or as a simple dessert. According to the late champion of southern foodways and culture Eugene Walter, some even consider it an ideal breakfast with ice-cold buttermilk and hot black coffee spiked with cognac. The elemental flavors of old-fashioned pones appeal to young eaters as well, so much so in the case of my two-year-old son that he has earned the nickname Tater Pone.

MAKES 6 SERVINGS

1 stick unsalted butter

$\frac{1}{2}$ cup sugar

$\frac{1}{2}$ cup sorghum molasses

3 large eggs

$\frac{1}{2}$ teaspoon kosher salt

$\frac{1}{2}$–1 teaspoon freshly ground black pepper (optional)

Zest and juice of 1 orange

1 teaspoon vanilla

1 cup whole milk

1 tablespoon brandy (optional)

3 $\frac{1}{2}$ cups peeled and grated sweet potatoes

Preheat the oven to 350°.

Melt the butter in a large cast-iron skillet. Pour the butter into a large bowl and whisk in all ingredients except the sweet potatoes until well combined. Fold in the grated sweet potatoes and pour the mixture back into the skillet.

Bake for about 1 hour, until well browned around the edges and on top. Let cool 15 minutes before serving.

Bourbon'd Sweet Potato Casserole

Holiday dinner planning often begins with this question: how are we topping the sweet potato casserole? It is a pretty heated debate, with folks offering to make the dish just so they can get their way. I stand firmly with the pecan streusel faction, but I want it crunchy and chock-full of nuts. Many families have settled the debate for good with this compromise: they top half with pecan streusel and half with marshmallows. If your family suffers from such turmoil, by all means, be a peacemaker. In mine, however, this does not really solve the problem because we have debated every aspect of sweet potato casserole until we are blue in the face. Should we include raisins, bourbon, or vanilla? How much sugar? We have thrown in the towel and just make two versions. This is mine. A shot of bourbon gives the dish backbone. It is considerably less sweet than my mother's version, yet far from austere. By slow roasting the sweet potatoes instead of boiling or microwaving them, you get natural sweetness and concentrated flavor, so less sugar is needed. You can even omit the sugar altogether, except for what is in the topping, if you desire. Once you scale back the decadence, this casserole is no longer reserved for special occasions but can become a regular at the dinner table alongside pork chops, pork tenderloin, or roasted chicken—and you can have Thanksgiving every day!

MAKES 6–8 SERVINGS

FOR THE SWEET POTATOES

3 cups mashed sweet potatoes (page 14)

1/2 cup sugar (or less)

2 large eggs

1/2 cup unsalted butter, at room temperature

2–3 tablespoons bourbon

Seeds and pulp from 1 vanilla bean

1/2 teaspoon kosher salt

1¼ cups chopped pecans
½ cup brown sugar
½ cup all-purpose flour
6 tablespoons unsalted butter, at room temperature
⅛ teaspoon ginger
½ teaspoon kosher salt

Preheat the oven to 350°.

In the bowl of a stand mixer, beat the mashed sweet potatoes, sugar, eggs, and butter until light and fluffy. Mix in the remaining ingredients and pour into a buttered 1½-quart casserole dish.

Mix together the topping ingredients and crumble over the sweet potatoes. Bake for about 40 minutes, until bubbly and golden brown. If the pecan topping gets too brown, cover it lightly with foil.

VARIATION ❋ Mama's Way: Omit the bourbon and vanilla. Increase the sugar to ¾ cup. Add ½ cup raisins. Bake for 20 minutes, then top with miniature marshmallows and bake until golden brown. (According to *Saveur* magazine, the first documented appearance of sweet potatoes baked with marshmallows on top was in 1917, when Angelus Marshmallows published a booklet of recipes designed to encourage home cooks to embrace marshmallows as an everyday ingredient.)

Roasted Sweet Potatoes and Crispy Kale

Have trouble getting enough greens in your diet? What if those greens tasted more like potato chips? That is exactly what you get when you roast kale (or collard or turnip or mustard or even sweet potato greens) in the oven. Combine the greens with sweet potatoes, which get sweet and caramelized when roasted at a low temperature, and you have a wholesome and compelling side dish for anything from burgers to roast chicken. Once you have this technique down, you will find the variations are endless. Experiment with different greens and spices and even other complementary vegetables. One tip: it is much easier to cut a raw sweet potato into uniform pieces if you shave a little off one side so the sweet potato lies flat on your cutting board.

MAKES 4–6 SERVINGS

---

3 medium sweet potatoes (about 1 1/2 pounds), preferably slender, unpeeled and scrubbed

4 shallots, sliced in half lengthwise

3 tablespoons extra-virgin olive oil

1 1/2 teaspoons kosher salt

1/2 teaspoon freshly ground black pepper

Big pinch of cumin

Pinch of cinnamon

Pinch of crushed red pepper

2 tablespoons sherry or red wine vinegar

1 teaspoon brown sugar

1 bunch of curly or red Russian kale, washed and torn into 2–3-inch pieces, thick stems discarded

2 garlic cloves, sliced lengthwise

Lemon wedges

Preheat the oven 350°.

Line a baking sheet with parchment paper. With a large, sharp chef's knife, slice the sweet potatoes in half lengthwise and cut each half in half crosswise. Cut each quarter into wedges 2–4 inches long and about 1 inch thick. Try to keep the wedges of fairly uniform thickness.

Place the sweet potatoes in a medium bowl with the shallots and toss with the olive oil, salt, pepper, cumin, cinnamon, crushed red pepper, vinegar, and brown sugar.

Spread the wedges out on the baking sheet and roast until the larger pieces are tender when pierced with a sharp paring knife, about 35 minutes. After 20 minutes, flip any that are getting too brown on the edges.

While the sweet potatoes are cooking, place the kale in the same bowl the sweet potatoes were in, along with the sliced garlic and a pinch of salt and pepper, but do not toss yet.

When the sweet potatoes are tender, remove the baking sheet from the oven and turn the oven down to 300°.

Toss the kale mixture with the oil left in the bowl from the sweet potatoes, adding another teaspoon if necessary to coat evenly. Spread the kale out over the sweet potatoes on the baking sheet. Return to the oven and bake until the kale is crisp, another 10–15 minutes. Transfer to a platter and serve hot, warm, or at room temperature with lemon wedges.

Company's Coming
Sweet Potato Gratin

Whether you call it a gratin or scalloped sweet potatoes, this is a handy dish to have in your repertoire. It is my favorite thing to bring to a potluck or family reunion. It looks impressive, is loved by all, and is infinitely adaptable. The sweet potato twist on a white potato classic is unexpected and makes the gratin even more versatile. Besides the sweet potatoes, cream, salt, and pepper, the spicing is up to you. I offer a cheesy version here and provide several variations below. You can also combine the sweet potatoes with other root vegetables, like turnips or parsnips, or add herbs for more variation. Just be sure the sweet potatoes are completely cooked before you pull the gratin out of the oven. If you have a mandoline or a food processor with a slicer attachment, this recipe is a breeze. If you want to make a lighter version, replace half of the cream with chicken stock or water instead of using lowfat milk or even half-and-half. Without the addition of flour, milk will curdle in the long cooking and ruin the dish.

MAKES 6 SERVINGS

---

6 medium sweet potatoes (about 3 pounds),
   peeled and sliced $1/8$ inch thick
Kosher salt and freshly ground black pepper
1 garlic clove
2 cups heavy cream
1 sprig rosemary
Freshly grated nutmeg
Pinch of cayenne
1 cup grated Gruyère or Comté

Preheat the oven to 400°. Butter a 9 × 13-inch baking dish.

Layer the sweet potatoes in the dish, sprinkling each layer with salt and pepper as you go.

Place the garlic clove on a cutting board and sprinkle it with salt. Chop and scrape it into a mushy paste. Place the garlic, cream, and rosemary sprig in a small saucepan and bring to a simmer. Season the cream mixture with a bit of nutmeg and the cayenne, remove the rosemary sprig, and pour over the sweet potatoes. Top with the grated cheese and cover with foil.

Bake for about 40 minutes, then remove the foil and bake until the sweet potatoes are completely tender when pierced with a sharp knife and deep golden brown, 25–30 minutes more. Let cool for 15 minutes before serving.

VARIATIONS ✳ Chipotle–Sweet Potato Gratin: Omit the garlic, rosemary, nutmeg, cayenne, and cheese. To the simmering cream, add 1½ tablespoons chopped canned chipotle peppers in adobo sauce.

Coffee and Sorghum–Glazed Sweet Potatoes: Omit the garlic, rosemary, cayenne, and cheese. Replace ½ cup of the cream with very strong coffee and add ⅓ cup sorghum molasses.

Ann Cashion's Sweet Potato Greens Spoonbread

As popular as sweet potatoes are in the South, the tender, nutritious leaves are relatively unexplored. More commonly used in Asian and African cuisine, they can be sautéed in a little oil and garlic, much like spinach or Swiss chard. An added boon is that sweet potato greens taste like spinach but do not contain oxalic acid, which is known to block the absorption of iron and irritate some people's teeth. Additionally, sweet potato greens thrive in the hot southern summer, whereas most other greens are cool-weather crops. They are popping up on chef's menus all over the Southeast as a wrapping for grilled fish, a substitute for grape leaves in dolmas, or just tender sautéed greens. They have recently shown up at my local farmers' market (a trend that is sure to spread), and you can ask any sweet potato farmer if they would be willing to sell you some. You can also find them in some Asian markets, but you can certainly substitute spinach if your search proves futile.

This recipe by Ann Cashion, James Beard Award–winning chef and Mississippi native, is an inspired twist on the old southern grits and greens tradition. Whether it is turnip greens and skillet cornbread, collard greens with corn dumplings, or this spoonbread, the mineral bite of southern-grown greens is a perfect match for corn's whispering sweetness. This creamy, luxurious spoonbread evokes sounds of enjoyment from diners and complements almost anything from brunch to supper. Use the best cornmeal you can find, and be sure to blanch and squeeze the greens well or the dish will end up soupy.

MAKES 6–8 SERVINGS

---

8 cups loosely packed sweet potato greens, trimmed with no more than 2 inches of stem remaining

3 cups milk

½ cup heavy cream

2 sticks unsalted butter

⅔ cup stone-ground cornmeal, preferably white
1 teaspoon sugar
Kosher salt
A dash or two of Tabasco
¼ cup olive oil
1 small red onion, cut in half lengthwise and thinly sliced
Freshly ground black pepper
2 teaspoons baking powder
4 large eggs

Preheat the oven to 300°.

Blanch the greens in salted water. Plunge in ice water to cool quickly and drain. Squeeze dry and chop coarsely.

In a 2-quart saucepan, bring the milk, cream, and butter to a simmer. Whisk in the cornmeal, the sugar, 2 teaspoons salt, and the Tabasco. Continue whisking while cooking over medium heat until the mixture thickens slightly, about 5 minutes. Set aside to cool while you sauté the greens.

In a 10-inch cast-iron skillet, heat the olive oil over medium heat and sauté the onions with a pinch of salt until soft and translucent, about 5 minutes. Add the chopped greens, another pinch of salt, and a few grindings of pepper. Stir to combine and add more salt and pepper to taste. Transfer the cooked greens to a medium bowl. Reserve the skillet.

Whisk the baking powder and eggs into the cornmeal mixture until well combined. Add about 1 cup of the mixture to the greens and gently stir. Pour the remaining cornmeal mixture into the skillet and top with the greens and cornmeal mixture. Use the back of a spoon to smooth the top.

Bake until set, 50–60 minutes. The spoonbread should no longer jiggle in the center when you gently shake the pan. Remove from the oven and serve hot directly from the skillet.

Impossibly Crisp Oven-Baked
Sweet Potato Fries with Chili Mayo

Sweet potato fries are popping up on menus across the country, and you can certainly make them at home (page 15). But let's face it, who wants to deal with the mess? Plus, oven-baked fries are healthier. The crispiest fries are achieved by soaking the raw sweet potatoes in cold water, adding a little cornstarch, and giving the fries plenty of room to cook on the baking sheet. If you are pressed for time, feel free to skip the rinsing step. Your fries will still be delicious! We eat these once a week at my house.

Sweet potato fries are known to inspire creative dipping sauces. Spicy Sriracha- or chipotle-laced mayo is a personal favorite, as is Indian-style tomato chutney. Ketchup is just fine, too, particularly if it is kicked up with a bit of harissa, hot sauce, or curry powder.

MAKES 4 SERVINGS

4 medium sweet potatoes (about 2 pounds), preferably
  a mix of varieties, unpeeled and scrubbed
Extra-virgin olive oil
2 tablespoons cornstarch
1 teaspoon kosher salt
$1/2$ teaspoon seasoning salt
$1/2$ teaspoon freshly ground black pepper
$1/2$ teaspoon cumin
Pinch of cayenne
1 tablespoon Sriracha
$1/2$ cup mayonnaise (or Greek yogurt)

With a large, sharp chef's knife, trim off a little of each sweet potato lengthwise so it will lay flat on the cutting board, then cut it lengthwise into ½-inch-thick slices. Stack a few of the slices and cut them into ½-inch-wide fries. Unless the sweet potatoes are longer than 6–7 inches, no need to cut the fries in half.

Place the sweet potatoes in a large bowl of cold water and swish them around. Drain the bowl and fill with cold water again. Let the fries soak for at least 30 minutes.

Preheat the oven to 400°.

Drain the sweet potatoes and dry them well between two dish towels.

Line 2 baking sheets with parchment paper. Drizzle generously with olive oil. Divide the well-dried sweet potatoes evenly between the two pans. Drizzle them with olive oil and sprinkle with cornstarch, salt, seasoning salt, pepper, cumin, and cayenne. Use your hands to toss them until they are evenly coated with the oil and spices and the cornstarch has dissolved. Spread the fries on the pans, being careful not to crowd them. For the most even cooking, place fatter fries around the edges.

Bake for 30–40 minutes, checking them after 20 minutes to rotate the pans from top to bottom so they cook more evenly and to flip the fries if they are getting too brown on the bottom.

To make the chili-laced mayonnaise, whisk the Sriracha into the mayonnaise.

Two-Cheese Sweet Potato Soufflé

This cross between a traditional French cheese soufflé and a sweet potato casserole is guaranteed to win over the sweet potato skeptic. It only takes a few extra minutes to whip the egg whites and create a truly spectacular dish. Do not be intimidated by making a soufflé. This one is equally delicious light and fluffy straight out of the oven or after it has fallen into a rich, cheesy custard. It is superb alongside juicy pork chops or in the spotlight, served simply with a green salad dressed in a sharp vinaigrette.

MAKES 6 SERVINGS

- ½ cup grated Parmesan, divided
- 2 tablespoons unsalted butter
- ½ cup grated onion
- 1 teaspoon finely grated lemon zest
- ½ teaspoon thyme leaves or finely minced rosemary
- 2 cups mashed sweet potatoes (page 14)
- ½ cup whole milk
- 1 teaspoon kosher salt
- ½ teaspoon freshly ground black pepper
- ½ cup shredded Gruyère
- 2 large eggs, separated
- 2 large egg whites

Preheat the oven to 425°. Butter a 1½-quart casserole dish and sprinkle lightly with 2 tablespoons of the Parmesan.

In a large saucepan over medium heat, melt the butter and sauté the onions with the lemon zest and thyme or rosemary for about 3 minutes. Stir in the mashed sweet potatoes, milk, salt, and pepper and heat until just warmed through. Remove from heat and stir in the remaining Parmesan, the Gruyère, and the 2 egg yolks.

Beat the 4 egg whites on high speed until stiff peaks form. Stir a third of the egg whites into the sweet potatoes to lighten the mixture, then fold in the remaining egg whites. Spoon into the prepared dish.

Bake for 20 minutes, then turn the oven down to 375° and bake about 20 minutes more. Do not open the oven door while baking. The soufflé should be puffed and dark golden brown with a nice crust on top when done.

Sweet Potatoes with Cumin-Buttermilk Raita and Lime

Around the time I started developing the recipes for this book, I was newly in love with the vegetarian cookbook Plenty *by London's Yotam Ottolenghi. On a particularly hot day at the end of summer, I found myself hungry and without a plan for lunch. As I stared blankly into the nearly empty refrigerator, I spied some buttermilk sauce left over from making* Plenty's *cover recipe for roasted eggplant the previous night. I thought of how old-timers speak of enjoying roasted sweet potatoes with a glass of cold buttermilk and decided to try the sauce slathered on one of the cold roasted sweet potatoes I kept in the refrigerator for testing recipes. I added toasted cumin seeds and the sauce reminded me of an Indian raita, so I sprinkled the dish with thinly sliced hot red peppers and some mint and cilantro. What a revelation!*

While a piping hot baked sweet potato and a glass of buttermilk may be the perfect autumn supper, with a different treatment, sweet potatoes can be just as appealing in the dog days of summer.

FOR THE CUMIN-BUTTERMILK RAITA

$\frac{1}{2}$ cup buttermilk

$\frac{1}{2}$ cup Greek yogurt, whole or 2%

$1\frac{1}{2}$ tablespoons olive oil

$1\frac{1}{2}$ garlic cloves, crushed and minced

$\frac{1}{2}$ teaspoon kosher salt

1 tablespoon cumin seeds, lightly toasted

FOR THE SWEET POTATOES

4 medium sweet potatoes (about 2 pounds),
   unpeeled and scrubbed

Extra-virgin olive oil

1 lime

Maldon sea salt

2 tablespoons chopped cilantro

2 tablespoons chopped mint

1 red jalapeño, seeded and chopped

Whisk together all the ingredients for the raita.

Bake or steam the sweet potatoes until tender (pages 14–15). Cool and slip off the skins. Slice into rounds and arrange on a platter. Place a dollop of raita on each slice, then drizzle with olive oil. Zest the lime directly over the sweet potatoes, then cut the lime in half and squeeze its juice over them. Sprinkle with the salt, cilantro, mint, and jalapeño. Refrigerate for about 1 hour before serving.

Sara Foster's Sweet Potato and Cranberry Salad

After enjoying a particularly scrumptious seasonal salad of roasted pumpkin and tart cranberries at Foster's Market in Chapel Hill, North Carolina, I asked owner Sara Foster for a sweet potato version to include in this book. Lucky for both of us, she kindly obliged. This salad is wonderful anytime, but it is especially welcome on those first fall days when the weather is still a bit warm for the rich, braised dishes of the season.

MAKES 4–6 SERVINGS

4 medium sweet potatoes (about 2 pounds),
    peeled and cut into wedges
½ cup extra-virgin olive oil, divided
Sea salt and freshly ground black pepper
3 sprigs thyme
3 sprigs rosemary
1 cup cranberries
2 tablespoons sherry vinegar
Zest and juice of 1 orange
1 shallot, minced
1 teaspoon honey
2 cups arugula
¼ cup chopped parsley

Preheat the oven to 400°.

Toss the sweet potatoes with 2 tablespoons of the olive oil and sea salt and pepper to taste. Remove the leaves from the thyme and rosemary sprigs, roughly chop them, and toss with the sweet potatoes. Spread in a single layer on a rimmed baking sheet and place in the oven to roast for 30–35 minutes, until the sweet potatoes are tender and golden brown around the edges.

While the sweet potatoes are roasting, rinse, drain, and pick through the cranberries, discarding any blemished berries. Toss with 1 tablespoon of the olive oil and season with sea salt and pepper. Spread evenly on a rimmed baking sheet and place in the oven to roast for 8–10 minutes, just until some of the cranberries begin to pop. Remove from the oven and allow to cool.

Meanwhile, combine the vinegar, orange zest and juice, shallot, and honey in a small bowl. Add the remaining olive oil in a thin, steady stream, whisking constantly. Season with sea salt and pepper.

Combine the sweet potatoes and cranberries in a large bowl with the arugula and parsley and season with sea salt and pepper. Pour the vinaigrette over and gently toss. Serve warm or refrigerate until ready to serve.

Crash-and-Smash Sweet Potatoes

This method of boiling sweet potatoes until tender, smashing them flat, and then roasting them produces lots of craggy edges that crisp up beautifully. Small or skinny sweet potatoes work particularly well when prepared this way.

MAKES 6 SERVINGS

About 2 pounds small, slender sweet potatoes,
    unpeeled and scrubbed
Kosher salt
4 tablespoons extra-virgin olive oil, melted unsalted butter,
    or duck fat
4 garlic cloves, chopped
Fresh thyme, sage, or rosemary
Freshly ground black pepper
Pinch or two of cayenne

Preheat the oven to 450°.

Place the sweet potatoes in a large, heavy saucepan and cover with cold water by about 2 inches. Season the water with 1½ tablespoons of salt. Cook the sweet potatoes until tender when pierced with a sharp knife.

Meanwhile, line a baking sheet with parchment paper or foil and coat generously with about half of the olive oil, melted butter, or duck fat. When the sweet potatoes are tender, drain them and place them on the baking sheet a couple of inches apart. Then, with a sturdy potato masher, a spatula, or the bottom of a small frying pan, squash the sweet potatoes. Brush them with the rest of the olive oil, melted butter, or duck fat, and sprinkle them generously with the garlic; thyme, sage, or rosemary; salt; pepper; and cayenne.

Bake for 20–25 minutes or until crispy and golden brown.

Mains, Soups, Stews, and In-Betweens

A WORLD OF FLAVOR

The recipes in this section demonstrate the versatility of the sweet potato in international cuisine. From the aromatically spiced North African tagines to the curries of Southeast Asia, sweet potato dishes are loved and valued around the world. The rest of the world utilizes sweet potatoes in savory cuisine more than the United States, as these recipes show. In traditional southern cooking, however, their suitability for savory dishes was also understood. Lest we forget, a favorite meal during colonial times was possum and sweet potatoes. While we may no longer have the taste for possum, you will find sweet potatoes a stellar addition to venison or beef roasts and stews of almost any kind. Sweet potatoes are marvelous flavor sponges and offer brilliant contrast to the spicy, smoky, and briny flavors represented in these recipes.

Clam, Ham, and "Yam" Chowder

Rules are meant to be broken, I suppose. I just could not resist this recipe title, but we all know I am talking about sweet potatoes and not true yams, right? Sweet potatoes love salt and smoke, so briny clams and country ham offer ideal counterparts. Tomatoes and wine add acidity, and the sweet potatoes soak up the mosaic of flavors. This dish is gorgeous, is fun to eat, and comes together quickly. Of all the recipes I developed for this book, this is hands-down my husband's favorite. One note of caution: the saltiness of the clams and ham will determine the overall saltiness of the dish. Beware of the salt you add via canned tomatoes or stock. You may not need any additional salt at all.

MAKES 4–6 SERVINGS

⅓ cup olive oil

4 ounces diced country ham or tasso

4 small dried red chilis or pinch of crushed red pepper

1 bay leaf

2 cups peeled and diced sweet potatoes

5 garlic cloves, minced

½ teaspoon kosher salt

½ cup dry white wine

1 cup chopped tomatoes (fresh or canned)

1½ cups low-sodium chicken stock, seafood stock, or water

¼ cup half-and-half

3 pounds manila or littleneck clams, scrubbed

½ teaspoon freshly ground black pepper

3 tablespoons chopped parsley

Heat the oil in a large skillet over medium heat. Add the ham, chilis or crushed red pepper, and bay leaf and cook, stirring frequently, for about 2 minutes.

Add the sweet potatoes, garlic, and salt and cook, stirring occasionally, until the sweet potatoes begin to soften a little, 6–8 minutes.

Add the wine and cook for about another minute. Add the tomatoes, stock, and half-and-half and bring to a simmer. Cover and cook until the sweet potatoes are tender when pierced with a paring knife. Add the clams, cover, and cook over high heat until the shells open, 6–8 minutes. Discard any clams that do not open and remove the chilis and bay leaf. Sprinkle the chowder with the pepper and parsley and serve with crusty bread.

Nancie McDermott's Vietnamese-Style Chicken and Sweet Potato Curry

When I began working on this book, I knew I wanted to include an aromatic Southeast Asian–style curry with sweet potatoes to showcase the sweet potato's savory side. I immediately contacted Nancie McDermott, whose cookbooks on everything from Thai and Vietnamese cuisine to southern cakes and pies are as easy to love as her own infectious enthusiasm. She shared this traditional chicken curry from Vietnam, where it is known as ca ri ga, *that will fill your home with the ambrosial fragrance of lemongrass and ginger as it bubbles away on your stove.*

MAKES 4 SERVINGS

FOR THE CHICKEN

- 2 tablespoons vegetable oil
- 1 tablespoon coarsely chopped garlic
- 1 cup sliced onions or shallots
- 2 stalks lemongrass, trimmed and cut into 2-inch lengths
- 5 slices ginger
- 3 tablespoons curry powder
- 1½ pounds bone-in chicken thighs or legs
  (or 1 pound boneless chicken thighs or breasts
  cut into bite-sized chunks)
- 2 tablespoons fish sauce
- 1 teaspoon sugar
- ½ teaspoon kosher salt
- 1 teaspoon crushed red pepper or chili-garlic sauce
- 2¾ cups chicken broth or water
- 1½ cups unsweetened coconut milk
- 2 medium sweet potatoes (about 1 pound),
  peeled and cut into 2-inch chunks

2 tablespoons kosher salt
2 tablespoons freshly ground black pepper
½ cup lime juice

In a large, deep saucepan or Dutch oven, heat the oil over medium-high heat for 1 minute. Add the garlic, onions or shallots, lemongrass, and ginger and toss well. Add the curry powder and cook, stirring often, until the herbs are fragrant and the onions are translucent, 1–2 minutes.

Add the chicken, spreading it out in one layer if you can, and cook for 1 minute. Toss well, and cook until the chicken changes color and begins to brown. Add the fish sauce, sugar, salt, and crushed red pepper and toss again. Add the broth or water and bring to a boil. Reduce the heat to maintain a lively simmer and cook for 10 minutes, stirring now and then.

Measure 2½ cups sweet potatoes and set aside any extra for another use. Add the sweet potatoes and coconut milk to the curry and simmer until the sweet potatoes are tender and the chicken is cooked, 10–15 minutes. Remove the lemongrass and ginger and transfer the curry to a serving bowl.

To make the dipping sauce, in a medium bowl, combine the salt, pepper, and lime juice and stir to dissolve the salt. Transfer to a small serving bowl. Serve the chicken hot or warm with the dipping sauce or simply stir 3 tablespoons lime juice into the curry after removing the lemongrass.

Lamb Tagine with Sweet Potatoes and Raisins

Sweet potatoes are common fare in North Africa, and they shine in slow-cooked North African roasted stews known as tagines, a term that refers to the conical clay cooking vessels in which they are cooked. Here, I substitute a heavy Dutch oven and simmer sweet potatoes with rich lamb in sweet and piquant spices until they are spoon tender.

This dish requires relatively little effort but tastes amazingly complex. I never tire of cooking or eating it. If you are not a fan of lamb, you can try it with pork shoulder or even venison. You can also easily substitute a boneless lamb shoulder for the shanks, but note that it will cook in less time.

MAKES 6 SERVINGS

- 6 pounds lamb shanks
- 2 teaspoons kosher salt, divided
- 1 1/2 teaspoons freshly ground black pepper, divided
- 3 tablespoons unsalted butter
- 3 large onions, halved lengthwise and sliced thick
- 2 garlic cloves, thinly sliced
- Pinch of saffron (optional)
- 2 cinnamon sticks
- 1 teaspoon cumin seeds
- 1 teaspoon ginger
- 1/2–1 teaspoon cayenne, to taste
- 1 cup golden raisins
- 1 cup raisins
- 1 (28-ounce) can diced tomatoes (or 3 1/2 cups chopped fresh tomatoes)
- 3 cups low-sodium chicken broth or water
- 3 medium sweet potatoes (about 1 1/2 pounds), peeled and cut into 2-inch chunks
- Handful of chopped flat-leaf parsley

Preheat the oven to 350°.

Season the lamb all over with 1 teaspoon each of the salt and pepper.

In a large Dutch oven, melt the butter and sauté the onions over medium heat. Season with a pinch of salt and continue to cook until the onions soften and begin to brown around the edges. Add the garlic, spices, cayenne, and remaining salt and pepper and cook for another minute. Add the raisins, tomatoes, and chicken broth or water and return to a lively simmer. Nestle the lamb shanks into the stew base and bake tightly covered for 1½ hours.

Remove from the oven and stir in the sweet potatoes. Bake covered for approximately 1½ hours or until the lamb and the sweet potatoes are meltingly tender. Remove the lid, raise the oven temperature to 425°, and bake for another 15 minutes to brown.

Skim off any excess fat, remove the cinnamon sticks, and scatter the parsley over the stew. Serve with crusty bread, buttered couscous, mashed potatoes, or grits.

TIP ✻ The best way to remove the excess fat from this dish is to make it a day ahead, refrigerate it overnight, and remove any congealed fat. Reheat to serve, then add the parsley. Like most stews, the flavor will only improve overnight in the refrigerator.

Shrimp and Sweet Potato Bisque

Seafood and sweet potatoes form the perfect partnership, but the pairing is rare—outside of South Louisiana, that is, where a plentiful supply of both can be found. This bisque has become a favorite of mine. It is complex enough for special occasions but simple and economical enough for every day. It is a perfect heavy hors d'oeurve served in small coffee cups. Although bisque recipes are often gloppy and taste of raw flour, the creaminess of the sweet potatoes means you can omit the flour altogether. The bite of the cayenne is delightful against the sweetness of the sweet potato, but you may reduce it to a pinch if you are sensitive to spices. You can always add more to taste.

MAKES ABOUT 6 SERVINGS

1 pound medium-to-large shrimp, peeled and deveined, shells reserved

6 tablespoons unsalted butter

2 cups chopped onions

1 tablespoon chopped garlic

1 bay leaf

$\frac{1}{4}$ cup chopped celery

3 medium sweet potatoes (about 1$\frac{1}{2}$ pounds), peeled and coarsely chopped

2 teaspoons kosher salt

Scant $\frac{1}{2}$ teaspoon cayenne

$\frac{1}{3}$ cup tomato paste

$\frac{1}{2}$ cup brandy, Cognac, or sherry

3 cups shrimp stock

2 cups half-and-half

$\frac{1}{2}$ teaspoon freshly ground white (or black) pepper

Place the shrimp shells in a stockpot with 4 cups water and bring to a simmer. Boil gently for 20 minutes, then strain, pressing on the shrimp shells to extract the most flavor.

Meanwhile, in a large saucepan, melt the butter. Sauté the shrimp until pink and just cooked through, about 4 minutes. Transfer to a plate with a slotted spoon.

Add the onions to the same saucepan and cook over medium heat until they are tender but not brown, about 4 minutes. Add the garlic, bay leaf, and celery and sauté another 2 minutes to soften. Add the sweet potatoes, salt, and cayenne.

Cover and sauté, stirring occasionally, until the sweet potatoes begin to brown just slightly, 3–4 minutes. If the mixture is sticking to the bottom or starting to burn, stir in a tablespoon or 2 of water. Stir in the tomato paste and cook another couple of minutes. Add the brandy and shrimp stock and cook until the sweet potatoes are completely tender.

Remove the bay leaf and stir in the cooked shrimp. Carefully purée the mixture in a blender or directly in the saucepan with an immersion blender. If you use a blender, remove the pour spout and cover with a kitchen towel to prevent the lid from popping off. For a velvety smooth bisque, strain the mixture through a fine-meshed sieve.

Add the half-and-half and white pepper and return to a gentle simmer for a few minutes. Taste and adjust the seasoning as necessary.

Sweet Potato Chiles Rellenos

Raleigh, North Carolina, chef Ashley Christensen is a gem. She had the guts to serve a twelve-course vegetarian lunch at the 2012 Southern Foodways Alliance symposium on barbecue that blew the self-proclaimed carnivores away. Of the many memorable dishes served, none wowed me more than her kuri squash chiles rellenos. Chiles rellenos can be grease bombs, but these were fresh and wholesome. Kuri squash can be difficult to find and cumbersome to prepare, so I developed this variation with sweet potatoes. While this recipe is a bit time-consuming, you can roast and stuff the peppers up to several days in advance so all you have to do is fry them before serving. You can even hold them warm in the oven for an hour or so after frying.

MAKES 4 SERVINGS

4 medium poblano peppers

3 cups mashed sweet potatoes (page 14)

2 tablespoons melted unsalted butter

$\frac{1}{2}$ teaspoon coriander

$\frac{1}{2}$ teaspoon cumin

Kosher salt and freshly ground black pepper

4 large eggs, separated, at room temperature

1 cup lard, peanut oil, or other vegetable oil for frying

Hot chowchow or salsa verde (page 82)

Over a gas burner or on a baking sheet placed under the broiler, blister and blacken the peppers all over. Use tongs to rotate them so they cook evenly. Place the blackened peppers in a large bowl and cover with plastic wrap to steam for 15 minutes, then scrape off the skins and discard them.

Working one at a time, lay each pepper on a cutting board with the stem pointing away from you. Open up the pepper by cutting down the center lengthwise from stem to tip, being careful not to cut all the way through, then make a second cut perpendicular to the first at the widest part about ½ inch from the stem, leaving the stem attached. Do not fret too much if you cut through one. Use a spoon to scrape out the seeds and membranes and discard them.

Season the mashed sweet potatoes with the butter, the spices, and salt and pepper to taste. Use a spoon to fill the cavities of the peppers with the seasoned mashed sweet potatoes and then close them up as well as possible. The peppers can be made ahead up to this point and held for several days in the refrigerator.

Whisk the egg yolks in a small bowl until frothy. Use a handheld mixer to beat the whites with ½ teaspoon salt until stiff peaks form. Gently fold the yolks into the whites.

Coat the stuffed peppers in the egg batter and fry in hot oil for 2–3 minutes on each side. Serve hot with chowchow or salsa verde.

Green Chili and Sweet Potato Tamales

My college love of a Delta boy gave rise to my love of tamales. His hometown of Greenville, Mississippi, may be the hot tamale capital, but we rarely made it there from Millsaps College in Jackson, Mississippi, before stopping at one of the gas stations or roadside stands hawking hot tamales along the way.

Years later, I found myself working in the largely Hispanic-staffed restaurant kitchens of Chapel Hill, North Carolina, where I amused my Mexican compañeros with tales of wet, coffee-filter-wrapped Mississippi tamales eaten on saltine crackers. No matter how poetically I waxed, they just shook their heads and repeated, "In Mississippi? On crackers?"

My love for the tamales of my native Mississippi is no cause for provincialism. Traditional Mexican tamales like these are easy to love and deserve some respect as the antecedent of those found at stands lining Highway 61. You can find masa harina for tamales, corn husks, salsa verde, and Mexican melting cheese, Chihuahua, in most Latino markets or in the Hispanic section of most grocery stores. If you would like to make your own salsa, the recipe below makes more than you need, but you will have no trouble finding other uses for it. This recipe is long but not at all difficult, and more than any other recipe in the book, it is completely worth it. A few extra hands make filling the corn husks a breeze, and whenever tamales are served, festivity commences.

MAKES ABOUT 6 SERVINGS

30 dried corn husks

FOR THE SALSA VERDE (MAKES ABOUT 2 CUPS)
1 pound tomatillos, husks removed
1–2 jalapeños
1/2 medium white onion, coarsely chopped
2 garlic cloves
1/2 teaspoon cumin

½ cup coarsely chopped cilantro
1½ teaspoons olive oil
½ teaspoon kosher salt, or to taste

FOR THE DOUGH
3½ cups masa harina for tamales
1 tablespoon kosher salt
2¼ teaspoons baking powder
½ cup plus 2 tablespoons lard or unsalted butter,
   at room temperature
About 3 cups chicken broth

FOR THE FILLING
3 large poblano peppers
3 cups mashed sweet potatoes (page 14)
2 tablespoons unsalted butter, at room temperature
½ teaspoon coriander
½ teaspoon kosher salt
Freshly ground black pepper
8 ounces Monterrey Jack or Chihuahua cheese,
   cut into 2 inch-by-½ inch batons
1 cup salsa verde

Soak the corn husks in warm water for 1–2 hours or until soft and pliable.

To make the salsa verde, preheat the broiler. Place the tomatillos, jalapeños, onion, and garlic on a rimmed baking sheet and roast about 4 inches under the broiler until the tomatillos blister and blacken in spots, about 5 minutes. Flip them over and roast another 4–5 minutes, until the jalapeños and tomatillos are splotchy-black all over. Seed the jalapeños for a milder salsa, if desired. Transfer to a food processor or blender. Add the cumin, cilantro, olive oil, and salt. Purée until you have a relatively smooth sauce with just a few chunks. Taste and add more salt if necessary.

To make the dough, combine the masa harina, salt, and baking powder in a medium bowl. Use your hands to knead in the lard or butter. With a wooden spoon, gradually beat in the chicken broth until you have the consistency of cookie dough. It should be very moist but not runny.

To make the filling, over a gas burner or on a baking sheet placed under the broiler, blister and blacken the poblanos all over. Use tongs to rotate them so they cook evenly. Place the blackened peppers in a large bowl and cover with plastic wrap to steam for 15 minutes, then scrape off the skins and discard them. Tear the roasted peppers into strips about 1 inch wide.

In a medium bowl, combine the mashed sweet potatoes with the butter, coriander, salt, and pepper to taste.

Form the tamales one at a time. Lay a corn husk flat in your palm with the tapered end toward you. With the back of a spoon, spread 2 tablespoons dough evenly over the husk, leaving at least a 2-inch border at the tapered end and a 1-inch border along the other sides. Dip the spoon in water to spread the dough without sticking to it. Spread 1 tablespoon mashed sweet potatoes in the center of the dough. Nestle a strip of cheese and a poblano strip in the center of the sweet potatoes and place a teaspoon of salsa verde on top. Wrap the sides of the husk toward the center, then fold up the bottom toward the center.

Place a steamer insert in the bottom of a big soup pot. If your insert is not as wide as the bottom of your pot, ball up foil to fill in the gaps. Pour water to just below the level of the steamer insert.

Place the tamales upright in the steamer with the open end at the top. Crowd them together so they support each other. Steam 1 hour over medium heat, adding more water as necessary to prevent the steamer from going dry. Serve hot.

Sweet Potato Hummus

In my family you would be hard-pressed to find a party food that is not chock-full of cheddar, cream cheese, or sour cream. This gorgeous sweet potato hummus is a fresh and nutritious alternative. It can be made several days ahead and refrigerated, but bring it to room temperature before serving for the fullest flavor. Serve it alongside warm pita and fresh vegetables like cucumbers and red bell peppers for scooping.

MAKES 3½ CUPS

3 cups mashed sweet potatoes (page 14)
1 garlic clove, smashed
2 tablespoons tahini
1 tablespoon lemon juice
½ teaspoon kosher salt, or to taste
¼ teaspoon freshly ground black pepper
¼ teaspoon cinnamon
¼ teaspoon cayenne
¼ teaspoon cumin
¼ cup extra-virgin olive oil, divided
2 tablespoons pine nuts
Sumac or paprika for garnish

Process the mashed sweet potatoes, garlic, tahini, lemon juice, and spices in a food processor until perfectly smooth. Drizzle in 2 tablespoons of the olive oil while the processor is running. Taste for seasoning and add more as necessary. If making the dip ahead, refrigerate at this point.

Transfer to a small serving dish. Heat the remaining 2 tablespoons of olive oil in a small skillet over medium heat. Add the pine nuts and stir constantly until they are fragrant and just golden. Spoon the oil and pine nuts over the sweet potato hummus and garnish with a light sprinkle of sumac or paprika.

Sweet Potato–Turkey Burgers with Creamy Feta Dipping Sauce

This recipe came about when I was making meatballs for a gluten-free dinner guest. I substituted some grated sweet potatoes left over from making latkes for the usual breadcrumbs. The recipe worked so well that I started adding grated sweet potatoes to meatloaf, salmon patties, and burgers. You can also use this recipe as a stuffing for bell peppers.

You can serve these turkey burgers with traditional fixings, but I serve them on a platter piled high with pita bread, cucumbers, tomatoes, carrots, and radishes with a bowl of creamy feta dip based on one from Jackson, Mississippi's, beloved Keifer's. It is like a tangy Greek take on blue cheese dressing. You can substitute Greek yogurt for part of the mayo in this recipe if you like.

MAKES 6 SERVINGS

FOR THE BURGERS

1 pound ground turkey

2 cups peeled and grated sweet potatoes

1 cup diced red onions

$\frac{1}{2}$ cup loosely packed chopped flat-leaf parsley

1 large egg, beaten

$\frac{1}{2}$ teaspoon cumin

$\frac{1}{2}$ teaspoon coriander

Pinch of cayenne

1 teaspoon kosher salt

Freshly ground black pepper to taste

2 tablespoons vegetable oil for frying

¾ cup mayonnaise
¼ cup red wine vinegar
3 tablespoons olive oil
1 garlic clove, finely minced
1 tablespoon Worcestershire sauce
Pinch of dried oregano
Pinch of cayenne
Pinch of freshly ground black pepper
1½ cups best-quality Greek feta cheese, crumbled

Preheat the oven to 400°.

To make the burgers, mix all ingredients except the oil in a large bowl and form into 4-ounce patties.

Heat the oil in a large skillet, preferably cast-iron, over medium-high heat and fry the patties for a couple of minutes on each side, until nice and brown. Transfer to a baking sheet lined with parchment paper or foil and bake for 15 minutes, or until the burgers reach an internal temperature of 165°.

To make the dip, whisk together all ingredients except for the feta until very smooth, then stir in the feta. You can make the dressing in a blender or food processor, but be sure not to over-process the feta. Add it last and pulse the machine on and off a few times to blend so the dressing remains a little chunky.

Sweet Potato–Tomato Soup
with Bacon Croutons

This simple recipe will solve your nothing-in-the-house weeknight dinner woes. It is healthy, quick, and easy and can be made from ingredients most of us have in our pantries. Sweet potatoes and tomatoes are a perfect pair. Sweet potatoes temper tomatoes' acidity by adding creaminess (without a speck of cream) and sweetness. If you do not have an immersion or stick blender, I suggest you buy one. No need to get a fancy one with numerous attachments or even a cordless model. I have the cheapest model out there, and it has served me well for years. Just be sure to keep your fingers away from the blade!

MAKES 4 SERVINGS

3 tablespoons olive oil

4 medium sweet potatoes (about 2 pounds),
    peeled and sliced 1 inch thick

1 onion, sliced

$1/_2$–1 teaspoon crushed red pepper

Kosher salt

1 (28-ounce) can whole tomatoes

3 cups water or chicken stock

Small bundle of sage leaves or pinch of dried thyme

1 tablespoon bacon grease

$1^1/_2$ cups diced stale bread

1 garlic clove, smashed (not chopped)

Freshly ground black pepper

Cream or crème fraiche (optional)

In a large, heavy saucepan, heat the olive oil. Add the sweet potatoes, onion, crushed red pepper, and 1½ teaspoons salt and sauté over medium heat, stirring often, until the onion softens, 4–5 minutes. Add the tomatoes, water or stock, and sage or thyme. Cover and simmer until the sweet potatoes are completely tender, about 20 minutes.

While the sweet potatoes cook, heat the bacon grease in a large skillet over medium heat. Toss the bread cubes in a bowl with the smashed garlic clove. Remove the garlic and discard. Sauté the bread cubes until golden brown on all sides. Sprinkle with salt and pepper.

Remove the sage from the sweet potatoes and discard. Purée the soup in the saucepan with an immersion blender or in batches in a blender. If using a blender, remove the pour spout and cover with a kitchen towel to prevent the buildup of steam from popping the lid off the blender. When the soup is back in the saucepan, season with pepper and add more salt to taste. If you prefer a very smooth soup, you can strain the mixture through a fine-meshed sieve (but I never do). Garnish each bowl of soup with a scattering of croutons and a drizzle of cream or crème fraiche, if desired.

Sweet Potato–Ricotta Gnocchi with Rich Shiitake Cream

I tried for years to find a successful sweet potato gnocchi recipe. They were all sticky, pasty, or as dense as bricks. This recipe yields light and tender pillows that need only a little butter and a dusting of grated Parmesan to shine. I cannot leave well enough alone, though, so I am sharing my favorite creamy mushroom sauce for them. I use shiitakes in the sauce, but regular white mushrooms will work too. This recipe should feed 4, but it is so good it might only feed 2.

MAKES 4 SERVINGS

FOR THE GNOCCHI
1½ cups mashed sweet potatoes (page 14)
6 ounces ricotta, drained overnight in a colander
½ cup grated Parmesan
3 tablespoons kosher salt, divided
¼ teaspoon freshly ground black pepper
½ teaspoon freshly grated nutmeg
Pinch of cayenne
1½ cups all-purpose flour

FOR THE SHIITAKE CREAM
4 tablespoons unsalted butter
½ pound shiitake mushrooms
¼ teaspoon kosher salt
Handful of thyme sprigs
3 tablespoons sherry
¼ cup cream
Gnocchi cooking water
Freshly ground black pepper
Parmesan

To make the gnocchi, in a large bowl, mix the mashed sweet potatoes and ricotta until there are no lumps. Whisk in the Parmesan, 1 tablespoon of the salt, the pepper, the nutmeg, and the cayenne. Mix in the flour a little at a time until a soft dough forms. You may have a little flour left over.

Turn the dough out onto a floured surface and divide into 3 equal pieces. With floured hands, roll each piece of dough into a long rope about 1 inch in diameter. Cut each rope into ½-inch-long segments. To shape the gnocchi, hold a fork in one hand and, with the thumb of the opposite hand, roll each segment over the tines of the fork to indent. The gnocchi should curl into a slight C shape with ridges along its back. Transfer to a baking sheet lined with parchment paper.

Season a large pot of water (3–4 quarts) with the remaining 2 tablespoons of salt and bring to a boil. Turn the water down to a simmer and cook the gnocchi until they float and are tender, about 5 minutes. Transfer to a platter or clean baking sheet with a slotted spoon to rest while you make the sauce. Reserve the cooking water. You can cook the gnocchi up to 4 hours ahead and simply reheat them in the sauce to serve.

To make the shiitake cream, heat the butter in a wide skillet and add the mushrooms. Sprinkle with the salt and throw in the thyme sprigs. Sauté until the mushrooms have given up their liquid and began to brown a bit, about 8 minutes. Deglaze the pan with the sherry, then stir in the cream and ½ cup of the gnocchi cooking water. Bring to a simmer and sprinkle generously with pepper. Taste for seasoning and add more salt or pepper as needed.

To serve, reheat the gnocchi gently in the sauce and divide among 4 bowls. You can add another splash of cooking water if the sauce is too thick. Top each serving with a couple of shavings of good Parmesan.

Shalom Y'all Sweet Potato–Apple Latkes

This recipe is inspired by one of my favorite people on earth. Many of my warmest memories, most stimulating conversations, and best meals have taken place in Marcie Cohen Ferris and her husband Bill Ferris's home in Chapel Hill. They are my North Carolina family. Marcie is an associate professor of American studies at the University of North Carolina at Chapel Hill and the author of the wonderfully titled Matzoh Ball Gumbo: Culinary Tales of the Jewish South, *where she weaves magical stories about growing up in the Jewish minority of Blytheville, Arkansas.*

Since settling in the great sweet potato state of North Carolina, Marcie has replaced white potatoes in her latkes, fried potato pancakes traditionally eaten at Hanukkah, with sweet potatoes. These latkes, developed by Miriam Rubin, are wonderful with applesauce, cranberry sauce, or sour cream and are too delicious to reserve only for Hanukkah. Try them with different sweet potato varieties. I particularly love them made with the All Purple or Stokes Purple variety, which has less moisture and cooks up nice and crisp.

MAKES ABOUT 6 SERVINGS

3 medium sweet potatoes (about 1½ pounds), peeled
1 large Granny Smith or Honey Crisp apple, unpeeled,
    cut into quarters and cored
3 scallions, thinly sliced
4 large eggs
¾ cup matzoh meal or all-purpose flour
1 teaspoon kosher salt
¾ teaspoon freshly ground black pepper
Canola oil for frying

Fit a food processor with the grating/shredding blade. Cut the sweet potatoes into pieces that will fit in the food processor's feed tube. Coarsely shred the sweet potatoes and apple. Transfer to a large bowl. Add the scallions, eggs, matzoh meal, salt, and pepper. Mix with your hands until the mixture is cohesive.

Using roughly ¼ cup of the mixture for each latke, press into patties about 3 inches in diameter, shaping them firmly but gently so they do not compact too much yet do not fall apart. Place the latkes on a sheet of foil or baking sheet.

Preheat the oven to 200°. In a large, heavy skillet over medium heat, heat 3 tablespoons oil until hot. Add 4–5 latkes; do not crowd the pan. Cook, turning once or twice, until nicely golden and crisp on both sides. (Watch carefully since these scorch easily.) Transfer the cooked latkes to paper towels to drain, then to a baking sheet to keep warm in the oven. Repeat with the remaining mixture, adding more oil to the skillet as needed. Serve warm.

Sweet Potato–Habanero Hot Sauce

I am a hot sauce connoisseur. Nowhere do I appreciate a great hot sauce more than at the breakfast table, where I drizzle it over fried eggs, home fries, and rich sausage gravy. I was dining on just such fare at Over Easy Café in Asheville, North Carolina, when my hot sauce request was answered with one of the finest concoctions I have ever eaten. It was a thick, bright orange Caribbean-style hot sauce fruity and fiery with habanero peppers tamped down with the natural sweetness of carrots. I decided sweet potatoes would be an improvement and set out to make my own version, which has been a constant in my refrigerator and on my table ever since. Habaneros have a delightful bright, citrusy flavor that is typically held hostage by their extreme heat. Most of that heat is in the seeds and membranes of the pepper, so step 1 is discarding those. Just be sure to wear gloves when handling them!

MAKES ABOUT 2½ PINTS

1½ tablespoons vegetable oil

1 large white onion, chopped

2 medium sweet potatoes (about 1 pound), peeled and sliced 1 inch thick

2 tablespoons chopped garlic

2 cups water

4–8 halved and seeded habanero or Scotch bonnet peppers

1 tablespoon kosher salt

1 teaspoon brown sugar

Zest and juice of 2 limes

¾ cup white vinegar

Heat the oil in a heavy saucepan over medium heat and sauté the onion until tender but not brown, 3–4 minutes. Add the sweet potatoes and garlic and sauté for another minute, stirring continuously. Add the water, peppers, salt, and brown sugar. Simmer covered until the sweet potatoes are falling-apart tender. Transfer the mixture to a blender, add the lime zest and juice and the vinegar, and purée until smooth. Store in the refrigerator, where it will keep for a couple of months.

Loaded Sweet Potato Skins, Your Way

When you sell hundreds of sweet potato scones a week, you roast a lot of sweet potatoes and are left with heaps of nutritious and delicious sweet potato skins. I would often snack on the skins, but one day I was inspired to create this recipe. These crispy, loaded sweet potato skins are so good they are worth making from scratch and figuring out what to do with the middles later!

MAKES 4–6 SERVINGS

6 medium, slender sweet potatoes, unpeeled, scrubbed, and baked (page 15)
2 tablespoons olive oil or melted unsalted butter
Kosher salt and freshly ground black pepper

FOR THE TOPPINGS
1 cup grated cheddar or other cheese
1 tablespoon chopped canned chipotles
1 cup sour cream
6 slices bacon, fried crisp and crumbled
2 scallions, thinly sliced

When the sweet potatoes are cool enough to handle, slice them in half lengthwise and use a spoon to carefully scoop out the flesh. Leave a ¼- to ½-inch border of sweet potato flesh to prevent puncturing the skin. Set the flesh aside for another use.

Brush the skins inside and out with the olive oil or melted butter and sprinkle all over with salt and pepper. Place on a baking sheet skin-side up and broil for 2–3 minutes until golden brown and crisp. Flip and broil the other side another 2–3 minutes.

Remove and top immediately with cheese. Broil for another minute if you want it bubbly. Stir the chipotles into the sour cream and dollop onto the skins. Top with the bacon and scallions.

VARIATIONS ✳ You can also top the skins with guacamole, bacon, and halved grape tomatoes; cheddar, chorizo, sour cream, and pickled jalapeños; or feta, pineapple, jalapeños, and cilantro.

Delta Bistro's Rainy Day Minestrone

Food writer John T. Edge named this dish by Taylor Bowen Rick-etts of Greenwood, Mississippi's, Delta Bistro one of his top ten dishes of 2012 for Garden & Gun Magazine. *He had this to say about it: "Sweet potato greens, grown and harvested by farmer Bonita Conwell in nearby Mound Bayou, make this dish. Con-jure a delicate cross between spinach, mustard, and purslane and you're close. As mucilaginous okra binds a great gumbo, those starchy greens, which some farmers appropriately call leaves, bind this minestrone. . . . Until recently, Conwell, and her collaborators at the Southern Rural Black Women's Initiative, froze those greens and shipped them to an African market in Houston. Thanks to Ricketts, some now remain in Mississippi and grace Delta stew pots. With a little luck, sweet potato greens will emerge as the next starlet vegetable, the watermelon radish of 2013."*

Ricketts says the keys to this dish are using really good stock and slow-cooking the vegetables in rich, aromatic fat. She gener-ally uses duck breasts, but I call for duck legs because they are more economical for home cooks. Either way, this recipe starts with long braising of the duck, which can be done days in advance.

MAKES 8 SERVINGS

4 whole duck legs (about 2½ pounds)

Kosher salt and freshly ground black pepper

2 sticks unsalted butter

Small bundle of thyme sprigs

2 bay leaves

½ pound bacon, diced

½ pound Andouille or venison sausage, diced

3 tablespoons sifted all-purpose flour or Wondra

1 cup chopped onions

½ cup chopped poblano peppers

¼ cup chopped celery

½ cup chopped carrots

2 tablespoons chopped garlic

1 medium sweet potato, peeled and chopped

6–7 cups chicken stock, preferably homemade, divided

1 cup chopped tomatoes

½ cup butterbeans, fresh or frozen

1 cup field peas, fresh or frozen (any mixture of
   black-eyed peas, purple-hull peas, etc.)

1 cup cut green beans, fresh or frozen

2 cups muscadine wine or other white wine

1½ cups chopped sweet potato greens (or spinach)

2 tablespoons apple cider vinegar

Pinch or two of cayenne

Freshly grated nutmeg

1 tablespoon chopped basil or ½ teaspoon dried

1 tablespoon chopped oregano or ½ teaspoon dried

Preheat the oven to 250°.

Season the duck with salt and pepper and place skin-side down in a Dutch oven with the butter, thyme sprigs, and bay leaves. Cover and bake for about 3 hours or until the meat easily pulls away from the bone. Remove the duck legs from the fat to cool. Measure ¼ cup of the fat, reserving the remaining fat for another use.

Coarsely shred the duck. Discard the bones and skin or fry the skin crisp to use as a garnish if desired. This step can be completed up to 7 days ahead.

In a large soup pot, fry the bacon slowly over low heat until it begins to brown, about 5 minutes. Add the sausage and cook another 5–10 minutes until the bacon and sausage are browned and have given up a good deal of their fat. With a slotted spoon, remove them to a plate.

Add ¼ cup duck fat to the bacon and sausage fat and turn heat to medium low. Sprinkle the fat with the flour. Stir constantly with a flat-edged wooden spoon until the flour is honey blond. Add the onions, peppers, celery, carrots, garlic, and sweet potato along with a couple pinches of salt and sauté until the onions are translucent, 5–7 minutes. Keep scraping the bottom of the pan.

Stir in 2 cups chicken stock along with the tomatoes, butterbeans, field peas, green beans, and bacon and sausage. Simmer for 15 minutes, adding a splash more chicken stock if the mixture gets too dry.

Slowly stir in 4 more cups of chicken stock along with the remaining ingredients and the reserved duck. Season with salt and pepper. Simmer very slowly for at least 1 hour, preferably 2. Taste and adjust seasoning as necessary. Serve with hot, crispy cornbread.

Desserts

A LITTLE SOMETHING SWEET

Most of the creativity with the sweet potato that I have witnessed has been in making desserts. The sweet tooth of southerners is legendary, and we live up to the claim. There is seldom a social gathering of any kind—from church supper to family reunion—where the dessert table is not as loaded as the dinner table. Cakes, pies, and puddings too numerous to name have crossed my lips, and many of them have featured sweet potatoes. In my hometown of Vardaman, Mississippi, we even have a specialty shop called Sweet Potato Sweets that ships desserts and confections made from Vardaman sweet potatoes nationwide. The recipes included here are personal, family, and career favorites, including the recipe for Sweet Potato–Ginger Crème Caramels that I created as the pastry chef of the award-winning Lantern Restaurant in Chapel Hill, North Carolina. Those crème caramels won the heart of my editor, Elaine Maisner, and got me the job of writing this book.

Sweet Potato Pie, Sister's Way

"American as apple pie" does not apply to the South. I did not eat my first homemade apple pie, or pumpkin pie for that matter, until I was an adult. I am from sweet potato pie country through and through. This recipe is for the sweet potato pie that most often graced our family table because my sister is the boss, and this is her favorite pie. Without a speck of spice, it stands in stark contrast to traditional pumpkin pies. Its simplicity is a revelation, which heretofore will call into question every pinch of cinnamon you sling. The sweetened condensed milk makes for a creamy, fluffy texture. If you buy ready-made pie shells, the recipe could not be easier. May we never see a store-bought pie at a potluck again!

MAKES 2 PIES

---

4 cups mashed sweet potatoes (page 14)
1 (14-ounce) can sweetened condensed milk
1 stick melted unsalted butter
4 large eggs, beaten
2 teaspoons vanilla
1 cup sugar
½ teaspoon kosher salt
2 unbaked 9-inch pie shells

Preheat the oven to 350°.

Whisk together all filling ingredients and divide evenly between the pie shells. Bake for 45 minutes or until slightly puffed and set in the center.

Let cool at least 1 hour before serving. Serve warm or at room temperature with very lightly sweetened whipped cream.

Sweet Potato Pie, My Way

This recipe is my version of a classic recipe I grew up eating in my mother's kitchen as well as at church suppers, family reunions, and festivals. It is spiced gently with lemon, vanilla, and cinnamon. I have replaced the more common canned evaporated milk and lemon extract with cream and lemon zest. A pinch of salt and a splash of bourbon make it better still. I also prebake my crust before adding the sweet potato filling to ensure that it is crispy and flaky in contrast to the rich and creamy filling. This recipe is fussier than my sister's, but it is worth it!

MAKES 1 PIE

2 cups mashed sweet potatoes (page 14)

½ cup sugar

¼ cup brown sugar

2 large eggs, beaten

¾ cup heavy cream

¼ cup milk

2 tablespoons melted unsalted butter

1 teaspoon finely grated lemon zest

1 teaspoon vanilla

½ teaspoon cinnamon

¼ teaspoon kosher salt

1 tablespoon bourbon (optional)

1 blind-baked 9-inch pie shell

Preheat the oven to 325°.

Purée all filling ingredients in a food processor until very smooth. Pour into the cooled pie shell and bake until slightly puffed and set in the center, about 1 hour.

Let cool at least 1 hour before serving. Serve warm or at room temperature with very lightly sweetened whipped cream.

Sweet Potato Bread Pudding with Whiskey Praline Sauce

This bread pudding was inspired by one at Damon Lapas's now-defunct Barbecue Joint in Chapel Hill, North Carolina. The Joint was one of those newfangled barbecue places where the seasonal specials, sides, and desserts are so good you forget about the barbecue. Some of my favorite dishes included pan-seared snapper with caper and herb butter, fried eggplant muffuletta, duck confit salad, and this bread pudding. Mark Hollar was the man behind this creation, and when I went searching for the recipe, I was told there was not one. After getting a few pointers from Damon and drawing on my memory, I created one that does it justice.

MAKES 8–10 SERVINGS

FOR THE BREAD PUDDING

7 cups stale bread (about 1 pound), crusts removed and
   cut into 1-inch cubes
2 medium sweet potatoes (about 1 pound), baked (page 15),
   peeled, and chunked
$\frac{1}{3}$ cup dried cranberries
5 large eggs
1 cup sugar
1 tablespoon vanilla
$\frac{1}{2}$ teaspoon freshly grated nutmeg
$\frac{1}{2}$ teaspoon cinnamon
$\frac{1}{2}$ teaspoon kosher salt
4 cups half-and-half
3 tablespoons melted unsalted butter

1 cup cream

¾ cup milk

1 cup light brown sugar

4 tablespoons unsalted butter

2 teaspoons cornstarch

3 tablespoons whiskey

1 cup toasted, chopped pecans

¼ teaspoon kosher salt

Butter a 9 × 13-inch baking dish, then layer the bread cubes, sweet potato chunks, and dried cranberries.

In a medium bowl, whisk the eggs until well blended. Whisk in the sugar, then add the vanilla, nutmeg, cinnamon, salt, half-and-half, and melted butter. Pour the custard over the bread mixture. Cover the dish with foil and let it soak a couple of hours or overnight in the refrigerator.

Preheat the oven to 350°. Remove the dish from the refrigerator and cut a few holes in the foil with a sharp knife. Bake until the bread pudding puffs up, about 40 minutes. Then remove the foil and bake for another 10 minutes until golden brown.

To make the sauce, heat the cream, milk, brown sugar, and butter in a medium saucepan until almost boiling. Meanwhile, mix the cornstarch and whiskey in a small bowl and stir it into the hot liquid. Boil gently for 1 minute until thickened and stir in the pecans and salt just before serving.

Serve the bread pudding hot, topped with the sauce. Unlike most desserts, this one reheats beautifully—even in the microwave.

Up-South Sweet Potato Cheesecake

I grew up with cheesecake out of a box topped with canned pie filling. My mother made many desserts from scratch, but cheesecake was never one of them. It did not belong to us, and we did not know any better. Real New York cheesecake is another thing entirely. It is impossibly tall and a study in contradictions—dense and rich yet light.

This recipe is the perfect marriage of two really good things: southern sweet potato pie and New York cheesecake. It is the kind of dessert you cannot resist shaving off slither after slither every time you open the refrigerator. The fact that it only gets better after a few days in the refrigerator makes it an ideal make-ahead holiday dessert—just be sure you hide it!

MAKES 12 SERVINGS

FOR THE CRUST

2 cups graham cracker crumbs

1 stick melted unsalted butter

¼ cup sugar

½ teaspoon cinnamon

¼ teaspoon kosher salt

FOR THE FILLING

2 pounds cream cheese, preferably Philadelphia, at room temperature

1½ cups sugar

1¾ cups mashed sweet potatoes (page 14)

4 large eggs

1 large egg yolk

1 teaspoon orange zest

1 teaspoon lemon zest

1 teaspoon vanilla

½ teaspoon kosher salt

½ teaspoon freshly grated nutmeg

Preheat the oven to 350°.

To make the crust, combine all of the ingredients in a medium bowl and press into the bottom and a few inches up the sides of a very lightly buttered 9½-inch springform pan. Place the pan in the freezer for 10–15 minutes, then bake for about 10 minutes. Remove from the oven and cool on a wire rack while you prepare the filling.

To make the filling, turn the oven up to 500°. Yes, really. Beat the cream cheese until very smooth, then beat in the remaining ingredients and pour the filling into the crust. The filling will come up to the top of the pan. If you have too much filling, you can bake the excess in a ramekin as a treat for the cook.

Set the cheesecake on a larger baking sheet to catch any drips and bake for about 12 minutes or until golden brown on top. Then turn the oven down to 200° and cook for about 1 hour, or until it is set around the edges but a bit wobbly in the center. Remove from the oven and place on a wire rack to cool.

Cool to room temperature, cover, and refrigerate for 8 hours or overnight before serving. This will keep for over a week in the refrigerator.

If the cheesecake cracks, you can repair it easily by spreading a thin layer of lightly sweetened sour cream over the top. Blackberries, cherries, and blueberries, either as a compote or fresh, can also be used as a topping.

Surry County Sweet Potato Sonker with Milk Dip

Sonker is a regional name for a deep-dish cobbler that is popular around Mount Airy, North Carolina. Peach and sweet potato are two favorite varieties. As with all cobblers, there are many variations. Some are cakelike, some are biscuit-topped, and some are topped with piecrust. My favorite version includes both a top and a bottom crust. The bottom crust poaches dumpling-like during cooking. A milk sauce, known locally as milk dip, is poured over the top of the cobbler as it bakes and caramelizes around the edges. Watch Les Blank's 1983 documentary Sprout Wings and Fly *about Surry County, North Carolina, fiddler Tommy Jarrell, and you will see Jarrell's girlfriend, Corinna Bowden, take a bubbling sonker out of the oven. Better yet, make your own to eat while you watch it!*

MAKES 8–10 SERVINGS

Enough dough for three 9-inch pies (store-bought is fine),
    divided in half

8 medium sweet potatoes (about 4 pounds), peeled

2 teaspoons salt

2 cups sugar

1/2 cup sorghum molasses

1/3 cup all-purpose flour

1 stick unsalted butter, at room temperature

1 1/2 cups sweet potato cooking water

3 cups milk, divided

2 tablespoons cornstarch

1/2 cup sugar

1 teaspoon vanilla

Line the bottom of a 9 × 13-inch baking dish with half the pie dough and refrigerate. If using store-bought pie rounds, piece together 1½ rounds to cover the bottom of the dish.

Place the whole sweet potatoes in a large, heavy saucepan or Dutch oven. Cover with cold water and season with the salt. Cover and simmer until the sweet potatoes are completely tender. Transfer the sweet potatoes to a plate. Reserve the cooking water. When cool, slice the sweet potatoes as thinly as possible without breaking them up.

Preheat the oven to 375°. Remove the baking dish from the refrigerator and layer the sliced sweet potatoes on top of the dough. In a medium bowl, mix the sugar, sorghum molasses, flour, and butter with 1½ cups of the cooking water and pour over the sweet potatoes. Use the remaining pie dough to form a lattice-top crust. Bake for about 40 minutes, or until brown.

In a medium saucepan, whisk ½ cup of the milk into the cornstarch until completely dissolved, then whisk in the remaining milk and the sugar. Boil gently for 1 minute to thicken, then remove from heat and add the vanilla.

When the sonker is golden brown, remove it from the oven, pour 2 cups of the milk dip over the whole thing, and cook for another 15 minutes or until caramelized around the edges and brown on top. Cool for at least 20 minutes before serving—the milk will continue to be absorbed and to thicken. Pass the remaining warm sauce in a small pitcher with the cobbler.

White Sweet Potato–Chestnut Pudding with Chocolate Sauce

I adore chestnuts almost as much as sweet potatoes. Chestnuts have a similar flavor to sweet potatoes, particularly the drier, white-fleshed varieties, such as Japanese sweet potatoes. It is said that at the turn of the century a squirrel could travel from Alabama to Maine on the limbs of chestnut trees without ever touching the ground. It is one of the great ecological tragedies of American history that the majestic American chestnut succumbed to blight and was almost completely wiped out by 1950. Great efforts are in the works to establish a blight-resistant American chestnut, but in the meantime, small, diversified farms like High Rock Farm in Rougemont, North Carolina, are growing hybrid Asian American varieties. The trees are much smaller than native American chestnuts, with substantially lower yields, but the chestnuts taste superb. I first developed this recipe as a pastry chef to utilize locally grown chestnuts, but they are still difficult to find. This version relies on imported chestnut purée, which can be found at gourmet markets or online. For even more chestnut flavor and to make the dish gluten-free, you can use chestnut flour in place of all-purpose flour.

MAKES 6–8 SERVINGS

FOR THE PUDDING
- 4 large eggs
- 1 cup light brown sugar
- 1/2 teaspoon kosher salt
- 1 cup mashed white-fleshed sweet potatoes (page 14), such as Japanese or O'Henry
- 1 cup chestnut purée or unsweetened chestnut paste
- 1 1/2 cups half-and-half
- 1/4 cup all-purpose flour or chestnut flour
- 4 tablespoons unsalted butter
- Seeds and pulp from 1 vanilla bean

¼ cup brandy or other brown liqueur
Powdered sugar

FOR THE CHOCOLATE SAUCE (MAKES ABOUT 2 CUPS)
1 cup water
1½ cups sugar
4 tablespoons light corn syrup or agave nectar
½ cup unsweetened cocoa powder
2 tablespoons unsalted butter
2 ounces semisweet chocolate, finely chopped
¼ teaspoon vanilla
Pinch of kosher salt

Preheat the oven to 375°.

To make the pudding, in a large bowl, beat the eggs with the brown sugar and salt until well combined. Whisk in the mashed sweet potatoes, chestnut purée or paste, and half-and-half. Fold in the flour. Melt the butter in a skillet until the foaming subsides and it begins to brown and smell toasty. Fold the seeds from the vanilla bean into the pudding along with the browned butter and brandy.

Butter a 1½-quart casserole and pour in the pudding. Bake for 30–35 minutes, until a knife inserted in the center comes out clean.

Meanwhile, to make the chocolate sauce, in a medium sauce-pan, whisk together the water, sugar, corn syrup or agave nectar, and cocoa powder and bring to a boil. Boil gently for 1 minute and remove from heat. Whisk in the butter, chocolate, vanilla, and salt. Let cool briefly to thicken. The sauce will keep for weeks in the refrigerator. Warm gently before serving.

Allow the pudding to cool for 20 minutes before serving. It will fall slightly. Sprinkle the pudding lightly with powdered sugar and serve it with warm chocolate sauce.

Sweet Potato Tarte Tatin

Want a dazzling dessert that showcases sweet potatoes simply but in an entirely new way? This is it. Caramel can be a little nerve-wracking to work with if you have never made it, but with a little patience, it is easily mastered. This tart is best served within several hours of making it. You can do as the French do and serve it with a dollop of crème fraiche, but no one will complain if you go all-American and serve it up with a big scoop of vanilla ice cream to sop up the luscious caramel.

MAKES 8 SERVINGS

1½ cups sugar

10 tablespoons unsalted butter

4 medium sweet potatoes (about 2 pounds),
  peeled and sliced ½ inch thick

¾ cup water

3 tablespoons lemon juice

¾ teaspoon kosher salt

Seeds and pulp from 1 vanilla bean

Circle of puff pastry 10½ inches in diameter

Preheat the oven to 425°. Line a baking sheet with parchment paper or foil.

Sprinkle the sugar evenly over the bottom of a 10-inch cast-iron skillet and dot with the butter.

Starting at the outside edge of the skillet, layer the sweet potato slices in a concentric circle. Crowd them so they are almost standing up in a neat overlapping pattern that covers the bottom of the pan.

Pour in the water and lemon juice and sprinkle with the salt. Scatter the seeds from the vanilla bean over the top and cover with a tight-fitting lid. Simmer over medium-low heat until the sweet potatoes are just tender, about 20 minutes. Remove the lid and cook until the excess water evaporates and the sugars begin to caramelize. Use a spoon to baste the sweet potatoes from time to time and gently shake the pan so they caramelize evenly. When the sugar reaches a dark golden color, remove the pan from the heat. You can drop a spoonful of caramel on a white plate to better gage the color if you are unsure. If the caramel seems to be darkening unevenly, use a spoon or silicone spatula to stir it.

Top the sweet potatoes with the puff pastry, pushing it down a bit to keep it in place. Place the skillet on the baking sheet to catch any spills and bake until golden brown on top, 20–25 minutes. Remove from the oven and let cool in the pan on a wire rack 15–20 minutes. Then place a large, rimmed platter over the top of the skillet and hold it firmly as you quickly but carefully invert it using oven mitts. Be very careful to avoid spilling the hot caramel. Serve hot or warm.

Sweet Potato–Rum Raisin Quickbread

I have a well-stocked liquor cabinet, but I rarely drink the hard stuff. I do, however, frequently use brown liquor in baking. The warming caramel notes counterbalance sweetness beautifully. Here, I take the extra step of plumping raisins in dark rum to turn familiar sweet potato quickbread into something festive.

MAKES 3 (1-POUND) LOAVES

1½ cups raisins

½ cup dark rum

2½ cups mashed sweet potatoes (page 14)

1 cup vegetable oil

1 teaspoon vanilla

4 large eggs

2½ cups sugar

3½ cups sifted unbleached all-purpose flour

2 teaspoons baking soda

1½ teaspoons kosher salt

2 teaspoons cinnamon

2 cups toasted and chopped walnuts

¼ cup turbinado sugar

Preheat the oven to 350°. Butter and flour 3 loaf pans.

Place the raisins in a small container and add the rum. Steep for at least 1 hour, tossing occasionally.

In a large bowl, whisk together the mashed sweet potatoes, oil, vanilla, eggs, and sugar.

In another bowl, whisk together the flour, baking soda, salt, and cinnamon. Whisk the flour mixture into the wet ingredients until just blended. Fold in the raisins (with the rum) and the walnuts. Divide the batter among the prepared pans and sprinkle with the turbinado sugar. Bake 45–50 minutes or until a cake tester comes out clean. Cool on a wire rack in the pans about 10 minutes, then gently remove from the pans and transfer to the wire rack to cool completely.

Sweet Potato–Ginger
Crème Caramels

This is a delicate and delicious alternative to sweet potato pie. Preparing the custards in individual ramekins makes them feel extra-special. I have made them in disposable aluminum tins by the hundreds for parties, including a Generation Next lunch at the 2007 Southern Foodways Alliance symposium, where University of North Carolina Press editor Elaine Maisner fell in love with them. Later, when we were discussing the possibility of my writing this book, she asked me more than once, "And you'll include the recipe for the crème caramels, right?" Without further ado, here it is.

MAKES 8 SERVINGS

FOR THE CARAMEL

3/4 cup sugar
1/4 cup water

FOR THE CUSTARD

1 cup milk
2 cups heavy cream
1/4 cup chopped ginger
2 (1-inch-wide) strips of orange zest, removed
    with a vegetable peeler
2 large eggs
1 large egg yolk
1 1/2 cups mashed sweet potatoes (page 14)
1/2 cup sugar
1/4 teaspoon kosher salt
1/8 teaspoon freshly grated nutmeg

Preheat the oven to 325°.

To make the caramel, combine the sugar and water in a small, heavy saucepan and cook over high heat, swirling the pan occasionally, until the sugar is a deep amber color, about 8 minutes. Immediately divide among the ramekins. Tilt the cups so the bottoms are evenly covered with caramel.

To make the custard, place the milk, cream, ginger, and orange zest in a medium saucepan and bring to a boil over medium-high heat. Cover and set aside to steep for 1 hour. Pour through a strainer and discard the solids.

Place the eggs, egg yolk, mashed sweet potatoes, sugar, salt, and nutmeg in a large bowl and mix to combine. Do not whip because you do not want to add too much air to your custard base. Add the cooled, strained milk and mix to combine.

Pour the custard through a strainer and discard any solids. Pour the strained custard into the prepared ramekins. Place the ramekins in a 9 × 13-inch baking dish. Add enough hot water to the dish to come halfway up the sides of the ramekins. Cover the dish with foil and vent by cutting several 1-inch slits in the top of the foil with a sharp knife. Transfer to the oven and bake until the custards are just set in the center, about 40 minutes. They should jiggle uniformly but not ripple. The custards should not puff or brown at all. Cool to room temperature and place plastic wrap directly on the surface. Refrigerate for at least 12 hours and up to 2 days before serving.

To serve, run a sharp knife around the edge of the ramekins to loosen and invert each custard onto a plate. Serve with a crisp cookie.

Sweet Potato Fried Pies

Fried pies, sometimes called mule ears, are a nearly forgotten old southern favorite. They were almost gone by the time I was making the family reunion circuit. Children of my generation usually passed them by for the newfangled Betty Crocker–type chocolate desserts, but my father gets misty-eyed when talking about them. They were the prized dessert of his childhood.

This recipe restores the fried pie to its original glory. A bit of lard in the crust produces incredibly flaky and easy-to-handle dough. Frying the pies in a cast-iron skillet in lard from pastured pigs produces a deeply satisfying flavor that cannot be replicated with cheap vegetable oil and a deep fryer. With simple farmstead recipes, using the highest-quality ingredients is essential. Only then can the tastes of our collective past be revived.

MAKES 12 HAND PIES

FOR THE PASTRY
- 1 cup unbleached all-purpose flour
- 1 cup unbleached pastry flour
- $1/2$ teaspoon kosher salt
- $1/2$ cup chilled lard, unsalted butter, or nonhydrogenated shortening, cut into small cubes
- $1/4$ cup ice water, plus a few extra teaspoons if needed

FOR THE FILLING
- 2 cups mashed sweet potatoes (page 14)
- $1/4$ cup sorghum molasses or brown sugar
- 1 tablespoon unsalted butter, at room temperature
- $1/2$ teaspoon kosher salt
- $1/4$ teaspoon allspice
- $1/2$ teaspoon cinnamon

- 1 quart vegetable oil or lard for frying

To make the pastry, combine the flours and salt in a large bowl. Add the lard, butter, or shortening and blend together with a pastry blender or 2 knives. Continue cutting the fat into the flour mixture until the texture resembles coarse meal. Add the cold water and mix it just until the dough starts to clump together. Add more water by the teaspoonful if needed to get the dough to come together in a ball. Being careful not to overwork the dough, gather it into a ball, flatten it into a disc, and wrap it in plastic wrap. Refrigerate for at least 1 hour.

To make the filling, mix the mashed sweet potatoes with the sorghum molasses or brown sugar, butter, salt, and spices in a medium bowl. Place in the refrigerator to cool completely.

Remove the dough from the refrigerator and let it sit for 5 minutes to make it pliable. Divide the disc into 12 balls. On a lightly floured surface, roll each ball into a 5–6-inch circle.

Place about 2 tablespoons of the filling in the center of each circle. Fold the dough over the filling create a half-moon shape and crimp the edges well with a fork that has been dipped in flour. Be sure that the edges are completely sealed. If the edges do not match up exactly, you can use a pizza cutter or paring knife to trim them. The pies can be frozen at this point and cooked frozen, if desired.

Fill a heavy Dutch oven or iron skillet about halfway with the vegetable oil or lard. Heat to 350°.

Carefully place the pies in the hot oil, making sure not to overcrowd the pan. When golden brown on one side, gently flip them with a slotted spatula or spoon. Cook until golden brown on both sides and remove to a wire rack to drain. Draining the pies on a rack makes them crisper than draining them on paper towels.

Repeat until all the pies are cooked. Adjust the heat as necessary to maintain the oil temperature at 350°.

I sometimes dust the finished pies with powdered sugar before serving, though my father does not approve. You decide. The pies are good warm or at room temperature.

Sweet Potato–Brown Butter Blondies

If ooey-gooey is your thing, these blondies are for you. In addition to the typical brown sugar flavor, these blondies have a healthy dose of sweet potatoes and spice. The sticky sweetness is balanced with toasty browned butter, and almond butter or peanut butter makes them extra chewy.

MAKES ABOUT 1 DOZEN

1 stick unsalted butter

2 tablespoons almond butter or peanut butter

1 cup light brown sugar

¾ cup mashed sweet potatoes (page 14)

1 tablespoon cinnamon

1 teaspoon ginger

1 teaspoon vanilla

1 large egg

¾ teaspoon kosher salt

½ cup all-purpose flour

1 cup chopped walnuts

½ cup toffee pieces

Preheat the oven to 350°. Butter and flour an 8 × 8-inch baking pan.

In a medium saucepan, melt the butter over medium heat. Watch it closely as it foams and then subsides. Keep it simmering until it begins to brown on the bottom and smells toasty. Remove from heat and let cool to just warm. Stir in the almond or peanut butter, brown sugar, mashed sweet potatoes, spices, vanilla, egg, and salt. Whisk well, then gently stir in the flour. Fold in the nuts and toffee pieces.

Pour into the baking pan and bake for 20–25 minutes, or until just set in the middle. Err on the side of underbaking. You want these gooey! Let cool completely on a wire rack before cutting and serving.

VARIATION ✳ Chestnut–Chocolate Chip Blondies: Use white or Japanese sweet potatoes. Omit the cinnamon, ginger, walnuts, and toffee pieces. Replace the all-purpose flour with chestnut flour and add 1 cup chocolate chips.

Sweet Potato Ice Cream with Toasted Marshmallow Swirl

Smooth ice cream contrasts with chewy marshmallow in this youthful take on marshmallow-topped sweet potato casserole. The whites left over from making the egg custard ice cream base are used to make a quick homemade marshmallow crème that you broil until slightly charred like a campfire marshmallow. You then stir this marshmallow crème into the ice cream at the end of the churning cycle. Summer and Thanksgiving collide!

MAKES 1 ½ QUARTS

FOR THE ICE CREAM BASE

2 cups half-and-half

1 cup cream

¼ cup brown sugar

2 cinnamon sticks

¼ teaspoon ginger

Zest of 1 lemon, cut into strips with a vegetable peeler

4 large egg yolks

¼ cup sugar

¼ teaspoon kosher salt

1 cup mashed sweet potatoes (page 14)

FOR THE MARSHMALLOW CRÈME

4 large egg whites

1 cup sugar

Seeds and pulp from 1 vanilla bean

Pinch of kosher salt

Bring the half-and-half, cream, brown sugar, spices, and lemon zest to a simmer in a medium saucepan over medium heat. Remove from heat, cover tightly, and set aside to steep for 30 minutes.

Place the egg yolks in a medium bowl and whisk in the sugar and salt. Whisk vigorously until the yolks lighten in color slightly, about 1 minute.

Remove the cinnamon and lemon zest from the cream, then slowly pour it into the egg mixture, whisking constantly.

Transfer the mixture back to the saucepan and cook over medium-low heat, stirring constantly, until the mixture coats the back of a spoon or reaches 170°. Remove from heat and whisk in the mashed sweet potatoes. Strain the mixture through a fine-meshed sieve into a clean bowl and refrigerate, stirring occasionally, until thoroughly chilled.

Meanwhile, prepare the marshmallow crème. In the bowl of a stand mixer or a stainless steel (or copper) bowl, combine the egg whites, sugar, seeds from the vanilla bean, and salt. Place over a saucepan of barely simmering water. Be sure that the bottom of the bowl does not touch the surface of the water. Whisk the egg whites constantly until they turn opaque, about 5 minutes. Remove from heat and beat with an electric mixer until stiff peaks form. Spread the mixture out on a baking sheet lined with parchment paper. Broil until slightly charred on the surface. Use a spatula to flip sections of the marshmallow crème and char the other side. It will not look pretty, but no worries.

Freeze the base according to manufacturer's instructions. When the ice cream is firm and almost ready, add the charred marshmallow crème by the tablespoonful with the machine running. Freeze another couple of hours in your freezer to harden before serving.

Sweet Potato Yum-Yum

My favorite desserts are of the cool and creamy variety. Anyone who has ever eaten sweet potato casserole straight out of the refrigerator knows that sweet potatoes have great potential in this category! Here I offer a sweet potato twist on banana pudding, featuring delicately spiced sweet potato custard layered with gingersnaps and topped with giant swoops of meringue. Bill Smith of Crook's Corner makes the best banana pudding on the planet, which is the basis for this recipe. He utilizes whole eggs in his pastry cream instead of just yolks, resulting in a lighter, fluffier pudding. However, you will have to crack extra eggs to get the whites you need for the meringue. You can use the extra yolks in another recipe.

MAKES 8–10 SERVINGS

FOR THE PUDDING

1 lemon

3$\frac{1}{2}$ cups half-and-half, divided

1 cinnamon stick

1 vanilla bean

5 tablespoons cornstarch

4 large eggs

1 cup sugar

Pinch of kosher salt

1 cup mashed sweet potatoes (page 14)

1 stick unsalted butter, at room temperature

3 medium sweet potatoes (about 1$\frac{1}{2}$ pounds), baked (page 15), peeled, and sliced $\frac{1}{2}$ inch thick

1 (1-pound) box of gingersnaps

5 large egg whites
½ cup plus 2 tablespoons sugar, divided
Pinch of cream of tartar
¼ teaspoon vanilla
Pinch of freshly grated nutmeg
Pinch of cinnamon

Wash the lemon in hot, soapy water and rinse well. With a vegetable peeler, remove the zest from the lemon in long strips from top to bottom, being careful not to get too much of the bitter white pith. Reserve the peeled lemon for another use.

In a medium saucepan, combine the lemon zest, 3 cups of the half-and-half, the cinnamon stick, and the vanilla bean, halved lengthwise. Bring the mixture to a very gentle boil over medium heat. Remove from heat, cover, and let steep for 1 hour.

In a 3-quart bowl, whisk the cornstarch into the remaining ½ cup of half-and-half until totally dissolved, then whisk in the eggs, sugar, and salt until very well combined.

Strain the steeped half-and-half directly into the cornstarch mixture and whisk to combine. Transfer back to the saucepan and place over medium-low heat. Stir constantly until the mixture registers 170° or thickens to coat the back of a spoon. Quickly remove from heat and whisk in the mashed sweet potatoes. If the mixture is lumpy or curdles, strain it through a fine to medium strainer into a bowl. Whisk in the butter a couple of tablespoons at a time. Be sure the butter is completely melted and blended well before proceeding.

Pour a cup of the custard into a trifle bowl or a 3-quart glass casserole or baking dish and coat the bottom and sides of the dish with it. Line the bottom of the dish and the sides with gingersnaps. Top with a third of the pudding mixture, then a layer of sliced, baked sweet potatoes, then another layer of gingersnaps, custard, and sweet potatoes. Finish with a third layer of gingersnaps and a thin layer of custard on top.

To make the meringue, preheat the oven to 325°. In the bowl of a stand mixer or a stainless steel (or copper) bowl, combine the egg whites and ½ cup of the sugar. Place over a saucepan of barely simmering water, making sure that the bottom of the bowl does not touch the surface of the water. Whisk the egg whites constantly until they turn opaque, about 5 minutes. Remove from heat, add the cream of tartar, and beat with an electric mixer until stiff peaks form. Whisk in the vanilla.

Top the pudding with the meringue, using the back of a spoon to make dramatic swirls, peaks, and spikes. Mix the remaining 2 tablespoons of sugar with the nutmeg and cinnamon and sprinkle over the meringue. Brown the meringue in the oven for 20–25 minutes or until the peaks are nice and toasty. Refrigerate for at least 1 hour and up to overnight so the custard soaks into the cookies.

Acknowledgments

As I was writing this book, family and friends shared numerous sweet potato memories and favorite dishes. I would especially like to thank my sister, Nicole Thomas, and my parents, Earl and Nita McGreger, for their insight. Other friends and colleagues provided specific recipes so I could share them with you. For that, I would like to thank Ann Cashion, Taylor Bowen Ricketts, Sara Foster, Virginia Willis, Marcie Cohen Ferris, Miriam Rubin, and Nancie McDermott.

I would also like to thank my husband, Phil Blank, who has always believed I had something to say, and my son, Moe, who brings me immeasurable joy as a dining companion and fellow lover of sweet potato pone.

Bibliography

Bower, Anne L., ed. *African American Foodways: Explorations of History and Culture.* Urbana: University of Illinois Press, 2007.

Brandon, Hembree. "Oppressive Immigration Laws Could Harm Mississippi's Sweet Potato Industry." *Delta Farm Press,* 22 Oct. 2012. http://deltafarmpress.com/government/oppressive-immigration-laws-could-harm-mississippi-s-sweet-potato-industry (accessed 25 Mar. 2013).

Bryan, Lettice. *The Kentucky Housewife.* Bedford, Mass.: Applewood Books, 1839.

Carver, George W. *How the Farmer Can Save His Sweet Potatoes and Ways of Preparing Them for the Table.* 4th ed. Bulletin no. 38. Tuskegee, Ala.: Tuskegee Institute Press, 1937.

Chapman, Jeff. "The Impact of the Potato." *History Magazine.* http://www.history-magazine.com/potato.html (accessed 28 Mar. 2013).

Dabney, Joseph E. *Smokehouse Ham, Spoon Bread, and Scuppernong Wine.* Nashville, Tenn.: Cumberland House, 1998.

Davidson, Alan. *The Oxford Companion to Food.* Edited by Tom Jaine. Oxford: Oxford University Press, 2006.

Denker, Joel. "Candy from the Field: The Sweet Potato, Part II." *The InTowner,* 11 June 2010. http://intowner.com/2010/06/11/candy-from-the-field-the-sweet-potato-%E2%80%93-part-ii/ (accessed 25 Mar. 2013).

Egerton, John. *Side Orders.* Atlanta: Peachtree Publishers, 1990.

Ellison, Ralph. *Invisible Man.* New York: Vintage International, 1995.

Fisher, Abby. *What Mrs. Fisher Knows about Old Southern Cooking.* 1881. Edited by Karen Hess. Bedford, Mass.: Applewood Books, 1995.

Fussell, Betty. *I Hear America Cooking: A Journey of Discovery from Alaska to Florida—The Cooks, the Recipes, and the Unique Flavors of Our National Cuisine.* New York: Elizabeth Sifton Books, Viking, 1986.

Jackson, Fatimah, Abdullah F. H. Muhammad, and Lorraine Niba. "Sweet Potatoes." In *The New Encyclopedia of Southern Culture,* vol. 7, *Foodways,* edited by John T. Edge and Charles R. Wilson, 260–70. Chapel Hill: University of North Carolina Press, 2007.

Kiple, Kenneth F., and Kriemhild C. Ornelas, eds. *The Cambridge World History of Food*. Cambridge: Cambridge University Press, 2000.

Lewis, Kerri Collins. "MSU Extension Launches Sweet Potato Challenge." Mississippi State University, Office of Agricultural Communications. Jan. 2014. http://msucares.com/news/releases/14/nr20140113_sweet_potatoe.html (accessed 2 Mar. 2014).

Louisiana Sweet Potato Commission, Louisiana Department of Agriculture and Forestry. *Louisiana Sweet Potatoes/Yams*. http://www.sweetpotato.org/ (accessed 15 Mar. 2013).

Lundy, Ronnie. *Shuck Beans, Stack Cakes, and Honest Fried Chicken*. New York: Atlantic Monthly Press, 1994.

Mann, Charles C. "How the Potato Changed the World." *Smithsonian Magazine*, Nov. 2011. http://www.smithsonianmag.com/history/how-the-potato-changed-the-world-108470605/ (accessed 25 Mar. 2013).

Mariani, John F. *The Encyclopedia of American Food and Drink*. New York: Lebhar-Friedman, 1999.

———. *The Dictionary of American Food and Drink*. New York: William Morrow, 2001.

Neal, Bill. *Biscuits, Spoonbread, and Sweet Potato Pie*. Chapel Hill: University of North Carolina Press, 1990.

North Carolina Sweet Potato Commission Foundation. *North Carolina Sweet Potatoes*. http://www.ncsweetpotatoes.com/ (accessed 15 Mar. 2013).

Olver, Lynne, ed. *The Food Timeline: History Notes: Pies and Pastry*. http://www.foodtimeline.org/foodpies.html#yamsandsweets (accessed 20 Mar. 2013).

Opie, Frederick Douglas. *Hog and Hominy: Soul Food from Africa to America*. New York: Columbia University Press, 2008.

Owsley, Frank L., and Harriet C. Owsley. "The Pattern of Migration and Settlement on the Southern Frontier." *Journal of Southern History* (1945): 147–76.

The Picayune Creole Cookbook, 9th ed. New York: Weathervane Books, 1989

The Pick of the Crop. Drew, Miss.: North Sunflower PTA, 1978.

Randolph, Mary. *The Virginia House-wife*. Edited by Karen Hess. Columbia: University of South Carolina Press, 1984.

Rhett, Blanche S. *Two Hundred Years of Charleston Cooking*. Edited by Lettie Gay. Columbia: University of South Carolina Press, 1976.

Roahen, Sara, and John T. Edge, eds. *The Southern Foodways Alliance Community Cookbook*. Athens: University of Georgia Press, 2010.

Robinson, Sallie Ann. *Gullah Home Cooking the Daufuskie Way*. Chapel Hill: University of North Carolina Press, 2003.

Root, Waverly. *Food: An Authoritative and Visual History*. New York: Smithmark, 1980.

Root, Waverly, and Richard De Rochemont. *Eating in America: A History*. New York: William Morrow, 1976.

Rubel, William. *The Magic of Fire: Hearth Cooking*. Berkeley: Ten Speed Press, 2002.

Schneider, Elizabeth. *Vegetables from Amaranth to Zucchini: The Essential Reference*. New York: William Morrow, 2001.

Smith, Andrew F. *Starving the South: How the North Won the Civil War*. New York: St. Martin's Press, 2011.

——, ed. *The Oxford Companion to American Food and Drink*. Oxford: Oxford University Press, 2007.

Snodgrass, Mary Ellen. *Encyclopedia of Kitchen History*. New York: Fitzroy Dearborn, 2004.

Stanard, Suzanne. "Researchers Reveal Sweet Potato as Weapon against Diabetes." North Carolina State University, *Perspectives Online: The Magazine of the College of Agriculture and Life Sciences* (Winter 2007). http://www.cals.ncsu.edu/agcomm/magazine/winter07/diabetes.html (accessed 15 Mar. 2013).

Taylor, Joe Gray. *Eating, Drinking, and Visiting in the South: An Informal History*. Baton Rouge: Louisiana State University Press, 2008.

Wang, Joy Y. "Last Chance Foods: A Rainbow of Sweet Potatoes." *WNYC*, New York Public Radio, 21 Oct. 2011. http://www.wnyc.org/story/166207-rainbow-sweet-potatoes/ (accessed 28 Mar. 2013).

Walter, Eugene. *The Happy Table of Eugene Walter: Southern Spirits in Food and Drink*. Edited by Donald Goodman and Thomas Head. Chapel Hill: University of North Carolina Press, 2011.

Warnes, Andrew. "The Uses of American Hunger." In *Hunger Overcome?*, 80–122. Athens: University of Georgia Press, 2004.

Index

CPSIA information can be obtained
at www.ICGtesting.com
Printed in the USA
LVHW011645070723
751844LV00008B/107